T0032792

BITING
THE
HAND

Growing Up Asian
in Black and White America

JULIA LEE

Henry Holt and Company
New York

Henry Holt and Company
Publishers since 1866
120 Broadway
New York, New York 10271
www.henryholt.com

Henry Holt® and Ⓗ® are registered trademarks of Macmillan
Publishing Group, LLC.

Library of Congress Cataloging-in-Publication Data is available.

ISBN: 9781250824677

Our books may be purchased in bulk for promotional,
educational, or business use. Please contact your local
bookseller or the Macmillan Corporate and Premium Sales
Department at (800) 221-7945, extension 5442, or by email at
MacmillanSpecialMarkets@macmillan.com.

First Edition 2023

Designed by Meryl Sussman Levavi

Printed in the United States of America

1   3   5   7   9   10   8   6   4   2

This is a work of nonfiction. Dialogue has been reconstructed to
the best of the author's ability. Some names have been changed,
along with potentially identifying characteristics.

BITING

THE

HAND

For my mother and father

Part I

RAGE

Chapter One

ANGRY LITTLE ASIAN GIRL

When I was in graduate school in the early 2000s, I took an intensive Latin course over the summer to fulfill my foreign language requirement. I was twenty-six years old and had just finished my first year of the PhD program in English at Harvard University. It had been a rough year, full of crushing self-doubt about whether I belonged in graduate school at all. That summer I lived on the first floor of an old Victorian house with no air-conditioning and a mouse problem that I discovered only after finding tiny turds in my toaster oven. Every morning, I walked the twenty minutes to campus to join a class of about fifteen students, mostly college kids and graduate students like me trying to pass our language exams. Our instructor was a balding white guy in his late twenties who was finishing up his doctoral degree in classics and fancied himself an amateur comedian. For three hours a day, he marched us through *Wheelock's Latin*, tossing in bad jokes when our attention flagged. One day, in the middle of a lesson, he cracked a joke that ended with a punch line about a dog (*canis*—the only Latin word I still remember) being taken to the back of a Korean restaurant and eaten.

The class laughed, and I felt myself turn hot with anger and shame. I was the only Asian person in the class. I did not smile, even after the teacher made eye contact with me and I saw his face tighten. *Shit, I forgot there was an Asian student in here.* I went home that day in a fury. I confided in some of my friends, who assured me I wasn't overreacting. The joke was racist, period. It never crossed my mind to confront the teacher. He was grading me, and I really, really needed to pass the class.

Instead, I went passive-aggressive. I put on my bright red ANGRY LITTLE ASIAN GIRL T-shirt and wore it to class the next day. On the front of my shirt was a cartoon of a scowling Asian girl, both her middle fingers raised. I'd bought the T-shirt earlier that year after stumbling across the Angry Little Asian Girl series online. Created by Lela Lee in 1994 while she was a student at Berkeley, the comic attacked the model minority myth, that hackneyed stereotype that Asian Americans are quiet, passive, acquiescent. Because Angry Little Asian Girl was "small and relatively cute," Lee wrote, people assumed she'd be sweet and polite. They were wrong. She was full of rage. She fought with her parents, clapped back at microaggressions, and swore a lot. The comic was a cult hit in the Asian American community, but when Lee tried to bring the series to television, she was told by network execs that her proposed show was "too racially charged" and that Asians weren't a strong enough consumer market.*

---

* See Anh Do, "Watch Out! Angry Little Girl Is Sharing Her Feelings," *Los Angeles Times*, April 25, 2013. In 2014, Mnet, an Asian American channel, broadcast two seasons of *Angry Little Asian Girl*; Lee voiced the title character; Margaret Cho voiced her mother.

Apparently, Angry Little Asian Girl was too angry, too little, and too Asian.

In retrospect, putting on the T-shirt was a dumb way to protest, but it was the only way I could tell my teacher "fuck you." Oddly enough, he got the message. Maybe it was my T-shirt, or maybe it was my death stare, but after class, he asked me to stay for a few minutes and apologized for his offensive joke. I could tell he wanted me to say it was no big deal, but I could barely look him in the eye. Walking to a coffee shop on Mass. Avenue afterward to get started on that day's Latin homework, I realized I was still trembling with anger. I did not forgive him. He had apologized only because he'd gotten caught.

* * *

I trace my birth as an Angry Little Asian Girl to the dawn of puberty. I hit adolescence at the same time my mother hit menopause. It was the late 1980s in Los Angeles, and while my parents worked long hours, I spent my time watching MTV music videos and calling in requests for George Michael and Terence Trent D'Arby from our landline. This was the era of sky-high bangs, Hammer pants, and Jordan high-tops, none of which my mom would let me have. Between the two of us and our raging hormones, there were screaming fights, some of them physical. I remember being eleven or twelve and talking back to my mom—maybe I wouldn't practice the piano, maybe I swore at her—and cowering in the laundry room as she pounded on the door with a rubber hose. Another time, she threw a full bottle of Sunny Delight at me. It missed me, landed on the floor, and exploded. She had a visceral hatred for our television set—we watched an appalling amount of TV while she and my father were at work—so she tried to smash the television set multiple times, finally busting it in such a way that no matter how hard my younger sister and I tried, we could get only black-and-white static.

My parents immigrated to the United States from Korea in the early 1970s. My dad had come here as a student, my mom as a nurse. But twenty years later they were now toiling at a fast-food restaurant called Pioneer Chicken, trying to sell enough wings and biscuits to stave off bankruptcy. My mom was less than five feet tall and never topped a hundred pounds. Yet I was physically frightened of her, even after I outgrew her. Her rage was incandescent. She was in her forties, stuck in an unhappy marriage, working long hours at a restaurant where employees stole from the register and customers threw corn on the cob in her face. The country was sliding into a recession, business was shitty, and now her oldest daughter was rebelling.

The irony is that everyone—I mean, *everyone*—thought my mom was absolutely adorable. I would watch strangers approach her and ask if she was Miyoshi Umeki, the Academy Award–winning Japanese actress who starred in *Sayonara* and *Flower Drum Song.* For years, I assumed this was a case of white people thinking all Asians look alike, but then I saw a photo of Umeki and gasped. She was a dead ringer for my mom, with the same pixie haircut, round cheeks, and impish smile.

My mom knew how to turn on the charm around strangers—usually white people, but also fellow Koreans. Partly it was about saving face. Called chae-myun, this code of behavior is common to many East Asian cultures and values harmony and honor. It's a kind of social armor. You might be broke or unemployed or depressed, but you cosplayed prosperity and success. For some Koreans, that meant driving luxury cars (even if you couldn't afford the payments), or mimicking a happy marriage (even if your husband was beating you), or bragging about your kid's straight A's (even if they were suicidal).

For my mother, chae-myun meant being decorous and polite in public, even when she was filled with roiling anger in private. It was far too shameful to reveal the truth behind the facade. To the outside world, we were a model minority family—quiet, undemanding, hardworking. But on the inside, we were falling apart.

Around this time, my father suffered a freak accident at work while trying to fix a broken oven. An employee had put a large pot of water to boil on the stovetop, and my dad jostled it while working on the oven underneath. The pot was a relic, with a bottom so warped it was more rounded than flat. It capsized onto my father, drenching him in scalding water. Despite the pain, my father dried himself off, changed his shirt, and kept working until closing time. Only then did he take himself to the emergency room, where he was diagnosed with first- and second-degree burns all over his face and body.

At first, my mother didn't tell us what happened, lying and saying that my dad was asleep in their room. We knew something was up, though, because the door was always locked and he never came out, not even for meals or work, and soon we were certain he was dying or already dead. When my mother finally let us in, my father was lying in bed, his body wrapped in gauze like a mummy. Half of his face and neck had been burned off, as well as most of his torso, and he was covered in raw pink ulcers that would later turn crusty and black. The room reeked of ointment. My sister and I cried, unable to hug him because the pressure was far too painful. In that moment, I felt anguish but also blooming shame. I tacitly understood we were not to mention my father's accident to anyone. It was too private, too grotesque. To our friends and acquaintances, we kept mum.

Not long after, my father returned to work. He had to. My mother couldn't run the restaurant by herself. He returned to Pioneer Chicken with a bandaged face, visibly marred to any customer who came in.

"What happened?" people asked him.

"An accident." My dad would shrug.

My father was stoic. Saving face even when his face was literally disfigured. Watching him, I felt my own face contort, trying to suppress a rage I did not yet understand.

* * *

I had always found refuge in school. I was an excellent student, eager to please and starved for the affirmation I didn't get at home. I was the kind of kid who diligently sharpened my pencils every night and joyfully picked out new binders and notebooks at the beginning of the school year. I dreaded weekends—two whole days stuck at home with no friends, no teachers, just my unhappy family.

When I was twelve, I started attending a private all-girls school located in a wealthy LA neighborhood straight out of a John Hughes movie. (In fact, *Pretty in Pink* was shot at a nearby mansion.) My father balked at the tuition, but my mother insisted they could make it work by practicing extreme frugality, cutting back on things like clothes, food, and health insurance. Driving through the neighborhood for the first time, I marveled at the wide streets, the stately Tudor homes, the massive lawns, so different from the shabby dingbat apartment buildings and bungalows in my own neighborhood. In my secondhand uniform, salvaged from the school's lost and found, and my saddle shoes, purchased two sizes too big to last longer, I felt like an impostor and clown.

My new school was cloistered and conservative, a legacy of its origins as a finishing school for the daughters of LA's white, Protestant elite. Though it had since rebranded itself as a college-prep school dedicated to empowering young women, it still clung to antiquated rituals like mother-daughter luncheons, father-daughter dances, and graduation ceremonies where girls wore white debutante dresses and carried bouquets. Of course, I didn't know any of this at the time. My mother just told me the school was for smart girls and that I was lucky to get in.

Over the next six years, my gratitude would sour into resentment and then a helpless rage. Where I had once been a teacher's pet, I soon developed a reputation for having a bad attitude and a problem with authority. Unlike my parents, I couldn't control my face in public. "When Julia participates in class, she makes it clear she wishes she were anywhere else," one teacher wrote on my report card. Another noted, "Julia has a negative attitude, but I am sadly getting used to it." I was called a wild card, someone who wasn't a team player. No one, it seemed, could understand why I acted this way—not my parents, not my teachers, not my classmates. What did I have to be so angry about?

* * *

In eighth grade, a year into my new school, my English class spent the year reading autobiographies and then writing our own personal essays. It's a familiar assignment to anyone who has been in an introductory English class, a seemingly straightforward way for teacher and student to get to know each other. The overarching theme for the year was "coming of age." Who were we? What was our identity? How were we transforming from girls into young women?

My teacher was a pear-shaped white woman with brown teeth and frizzy hair named Mrs. Church. Mrs. Church's favorite thing to tell me was "take a chill pill." That year, I was obsessed with the TV show *American Gladiators* and went to a taping at Universal Studios with my friends, where I screamed my undying love for Nitro from the bleachers. I was so extra, so emotional, so hyper—basically, an average thirteen-year-old girl.

I'd always loved reading, but eighth grade was the year I discovered I loved writing. In particular, I loved writing about things that made me angry, which encompassed everything from my algebra teacher to the Ku Klux Klan, the topic of my final research paper. We had read Charlotte Brontë's *Jane Eyre* that year, and I could easily identify with Jane's rebelliousness. The novel traces the life of Jane, a young orphan, from a miserable childhood living with her aunt and cousins to her grim education at a charity school to her employment as a governess in the household of a brooding master. For the narrator, Jane, writing her autobiography allowed not only a measure of release but also a measure of revenge. Jane might have been "poor, obscure, plain, and little," but she was also an angry little English girl. Writing *Jane Eyre* was how she got back at everyone who had wronged her—her mean aunt Reed, her stupid cousin John, the tyrannical schoolmaster Mr. Brocklehurst, even the manipulative Rochester.

I wrote two autobiographical essays for Mrs. Church that year. Both were filled with rage. But only one got a positive response.

The first essay was about being Korean American and how I felt torn between my parents' culture and American (i.e., white) culture. I wrote about how I wasn't good at math, how I fought constantly with my mother, and how I didn't even like kimchi. The last part was a lie, a detail I fabricated to emphasize just how un-Korean I was. In retrospect, it makes me cringe. I actually love kimchi, but I was so determined to reject all things Korean and embrace all things American that I was willing to perform, to *fake* disgust in order to emphasize how unique and unstereotypically Asian I was.

Mrs. Church loved the essay. She gave me an A and asked to show it to our head of school, a blond helmet-haired woman who wore skirt suits and looked like a Republican lawmaker. Mrs. Church thought it would help provide insight into the assimilation struggles of young Asian American girls at the school. I was thrilled. I'd always been jealous of Mrs. Church's favoritism of a white girl a year ahead of me, a girl who was a widely admired writer; who was beautiful, rich, and snobby; who would later go to a fancy Ivy League school, where she was a legacy. I saw this girl as my competition, even if she didn't know that I existed. *I* was a good writer, too. *I* had important things to say, too.

When our next essay was assigned, I got cocky. Mrs. Church's approval was like a shot of adrenaline. I suddenly felt powerful, brave, like someone who could harness words to speak truth to power. People in authority *wanted* to hear from me. I had access to the head of school's ear!

Emboldened, I decided to write a screed on what I saw as the obvious race and class hierarchy at our school. Of course, I didn't use those words. Instead, I wrote about how the "popular girls" at our school were invariably white and wealthy and (often) blond. I ranted about how they breezed through life, how they didn't bother to befriend those of us who were brown or Black or on financial aid, how they excluded us from their cliques and parties. It was an easy piece to write because it felt so true. How could anyone not see what I was describing? I was sure Mrs. Church would love it and would again ask permission to show it to our head of school.

I was devastated when Mrs. Church returned the essay to me with a B (which I thought was a punitive grade) and comments that it was poorly argued, overly emotional, and unconvincing. *What?* I thought to myself, feeling sick to my stomach. At that point, I was still ravenous for teacher approval. I knew I'd gone too far. I'd let my passion get the better of me and produced an essay that was full of unwelcome, misdirected rage. Maybe my writing was crappy, after all.

For a long time, I believed that this essay was a failure of thought and execution. I no longer have a copy of it, so I have no way of knowing if Mrs. Church was right and the essay was sloppy and weak. I've since taught high school English myself, and I know well how students can think they've written something brilliant yet be blind to its flaws. I also know how memory can play tricks. Maybe I got a B+. Maybe Mrs. Church wasn't as critical as I remember.

But the more I think about it, the more I'm convinced it was the *target* of my anger that so unnerved Mrs. Church. In the first essay, my rage was directed at my mother and cultural expectations of what it meant to be a good little Asian girl. The enemy, in my mind, was Korean values (patriarchy, stoicism) and racial stereotyping (Asians as compliant and good at math). In the second essay, my rage was directed squarely at white supremacy. Why did the white girls in my class enjoy so much privilege? Why did no one want to talk about it?

Back then, I had the words to describe the struggle of assimilation. We'd read Jeanne Wakatsuki Houston's *Farewell to Manzanar* that year, and I'd felt a pang of recognition at Houston's attempts to fit into white American society. Assimilation was something Mrs. Church—and by extension, white America—heartily endorsed. It required minoritized Black and brown populations to merge into the white majority mainstream. By raging against my mother and Korean cultural values, I was proving how American I was.

I did not yet have the words to describe the struggle against white supremacy. Nor did I understand that the model minority myth I so disdained was itself a tool of white supremacy. In my mind, Mrs. Church was one of the good guys. A nice white teacher helping her student speak out against oppressive Asian culture, plucking her essay from class as representative of the experience of Asian American students and serving it up to the head of school. Treating her like a token.

But with the second essay, I'd bitten the hand that fed me. I'd gone too far, too harshly, and directly indicted whiteness. Mrs. Church was white. She was not rich—her teeth betrayed her class status—but her racial identity trumped her class identity. At least that's what I suspected, then and now. My anger had repelled her. I did not show enough equanimity. I was making it about race when it was much more complicated and nuanced than that.

So why were we reading *Jane Eyre* in this class? Jane was a moody, depressed, and rebellious heroine. She fought with her aunt and cousins. She talked back to Mr. Brocklehurst. She hated the beautiful, rich, snobby Blanche Ingram. Yet here we were in 1990, reading it at an all-girls school, elevating it as a proto-feminist text. Look at how defiant and passionate Jane was! How willing to stand up to injustice!

An angry little English girl was a role model. An angry little Asian girl was not.

Maybe I needed to take a chill pill.

Chapter Two

THE RACIAL IMAGINARY

When I was little, my paternal grandfather, a widower, took care of my younger sister and me while my parents were at work. We lived in a small house near Palms, with an unfinished garage covered in bright orange shag carpeting. My sister and I would take turns riding around on our tricycle while my grandfather sat on the carpet, reading the Korean newspaper, drinking RC Cola, and feeding us bits of filefish he'd roasted in the oven. My first language was Korean. My grandfather spoke no English, and neither did we. Our world was tightly circumscribed and safe, a five-person pod bound together by blood, language, and culture. There was no need to venture out, no need to figure out who I was in relation to outsiders.

That changed once I started nursery school at age three. My grandfather was planning to return to Korea, and soon there would no longer be anyone to watch us at home. On the first day of school, my mom says that I cried and clung to her, begging her not to leave me. She left me sobbing in the sandbox, and when she picked me up at the end of the day, I was still sitting in the trough, pushing sand. The teachers told my mom I hadn't spoken a word or moved all day. I'd spent hours shoveling sand into my bucket and dumping it out.

My parents were worried. I was usually chatty and out-going, so my retreat into silence concerned them. When my sister, who was eighteen months younger, began nurs-ery school a short time later, she, too, stopped talking, and for such a prolonged time that the teachers thought she had selective mutism. She would rather wet herself than ask to use the bathroom.

My parents decided to start speaking English at home in the hopes this would allow us to adapt more easily. Their plan worked too well. Soon, all my sister and I wanted to speak was English. With my grandfather gone, we refused to speak Korean at home and lost the language in a matter of months. I remember one of my parents' friends coming over and asking me "How old are you?" in Korean. I stared back, uncomprehending, and guessed, "Um, Julia?" My mom was horrified. She had just wanted to help us assimilate, and in a flash, we were irretrievably Americanized.

Not long after, I came home from school and asked my mother, "Are we Chinese or Japanese?" A white classmate had asked me that question earlier in the day, and I hadn't known how to respond because I didn't know "what" we were. On the playground, I often sang a popular nursery rhyme that started with "I went to a Chinese restaurant" and ended with "Chinese, Japanese, Indian Chief." I pulled my eyelids up for "Chinese," down for "Japanese," and crossed my arms for "Indian Chief." Until then, I found the song catchy and amusing, right down to the hand gestures. Now, I suddenly saw myself through my classmate's eyes.

Wait a second, was *this* what she saw when she looked at me? Did this mean *I* was Chinese/Japanese/Indian Chief?

For the first time, I was experiencing what W. E. B. Du Bois famously called "double consciousness," that sense of "always looking at oneself through the eyes of others" experienced by people of color in a white supremacist society. It's an odd feeling of dissociation and splitting, of being trapped between the white gaze and your own. For Du Bois, the white world saw him as "Black," a distillation of racial stereotypes and presumed inferiority entirely at odds with his own sense of self and humanity. I was not Black, but I, too, had been slotted in a category of racial other, and I, too, felt a splitting, a fault line in my sense of self. Who was I? Or rather, *what* was I? What did white people see when they looked at me?

When my mother informed me that we were Korean, I felt a strange impatience mixed with anxiety. I wanted to report back to my friend with a simple answer. Yes, we were Chinese; no, we were not Japanese—or vice versa. How was I supposed to explain "Korean" to my classmate? My mom launched into a long description of Korea being a "peninsula," blah blah blah, and I thought, *That's not what my friend is asking. I can't tell her I'm a peninsula.* Frustrated, I resorted to tragicomic ways to make myself legible to the white gaze. At Korean school, my friends and I updated the nursery rhyme by wedging "Korean" between "Chinese" and "Japanese" and pulling our eyelids sideways. It didn't cross our minds that we were distorting our features to make ourselves visible to American culture. We just wanted to be seen, even if the image was warped.

I'd taken my first steps into what Claudia Rankine calls "the racial imaginary," a circus fun house world where I was no longer Julia Lee who lived on Richland Avenue with her mom and dad and sister and grandpa. I was now a little Asian girl, thrown against what Zora Neale Hurston calls a "sharp white background." Already, I was learning the rules of this world through nursery rhymes and my interactions with classmates. I was contorting myself in grotesque ways to be seen and to maintain a stable sense of self. Where I had once imagined myself full of detail and nuance, I now felt those qualities fading away, turning me into a simulacrum, a caricature, a paper cutout.

* * *

My parents were part of a wave of Korean immigrants who moved to the United States in the years following the Hart-Celler Act of 1965, which relaxed national-origin quotas that had effectively banned almost all immigration from Asia for the past sixty years. My father arrived on a student visa in 1970, traveling on a cargo ship (he was literally FOB) that docked in Long Beach after a monthlong crossing. He arrived broke, crashing in Koreatown with an acquaintance and finding work scrubbing toilets in Beverly Hills. (To this day, he recalls his amazement at the Trumpian gold fixtures in some of the bathrooms.) After a few months, my father had saved enough money to fly to Missouri and start classes at Northwest Missouri State University in Maryville, where he'd been admitted as an international student.

My father's academic career was short-lived. He ran out of money after two semesters and was forced to drop out of school. He moved to Philadelphia, where a friend lived, to find work. Having overstayed his visa, he took whatever job he could find. He washed dishes at an Italian restaurant (where he had spaghetti and meatballs for the first time) and worked as an elevator operator in a downtown office building. Walking past a Greyhound Station one day, he was stopped (aka racially profiled) by a plainclothes immigration official who asked for his papers and then cited him for working illegally on an expired visa. My father was ordered to appear before an immigration judge, the first step in the deportation process. Panicked, he reached out to an immigration lawyer, whose office happened to be in the building where my father worked and who had once handed him a business card "just in case." The lawyer represented my father pro bono and managed to buy him some time to get back into compliance.

My mother had a more privileged immigration passage. She'd earned a nursing degree in Korea and been hired to work as a *Gastarbeiter*, or "guest worker," in Germany. After a two-year stint in Tübingen, she was recruited to come to the United States and began working at a hospital in New Jersey. By then, she was in her early thirties (an old maid!) and part of a small community of Korean immigrants in the New Jersey/Philly area. She also possessed that magical piece of paper: a green card. A friend set her up with my about-to-be-deported father, and three weeks after their first meeting, they married at a Catholic church in New Jersey. In their wedding photos, they look stunned and sweaty, my mother in a homemade wedding gown with her makeup (too-white foundation, pastel eyeshadow) sliding off her face, my father in a rented tux and white gloves. Neither of their families attended the ceremony.

While my mother continued to work at the hospital, my

father found a job as a machinist at the Campbell Soup factory in Camden, New Jersey. He came home one day with a huge gash on his face, the result of a workplace accident, and my mother insisted he quit. They were planning to move, anyway—my father wanted to return to Los Angeles, with its warm weather, growing Korean population, and promise of better job opportunities. In 1974, a year into their marriage, they made the leap, driving cross-country in a lime-green Chevy Impala that looked like its ass was dragging because my mom had insisted on bringing her potted plants with her, only to have them confiscated by agricultural authorities at the Nevada-California border. They moved into a small apartment next to the 10 freeway, and my mother quickly found a job at Brotman Memorial Hospital in Culver City. My father started working at a local factory that manufactured industrial sealants.

Shortly after settling in LA, my father reconnected with an old buddy, a fellow college dropout who owned a successful liquor store in Pasadena and told him he could make more money working for himself. My father knew that with his limited English and lack of education, he'd be relegated to minimum-wage, dead-end factory jobs. With his friend's help, he applied for a Small Business Administration loan for minorities and bought a liquor store in a neighborhood called Inglewood. It was 1975, and the neighborhood was in the middle of a massive demographic shift. For years, Inglewood had been a predominantly white neighborhood (it was a Klan hot spot in the 1920s), but after the 1965 Watts Uprising, white residents began abandoning the area. White flight accelerated with the passage of the Fair Housing Act of 1968, which dismantled discriminatory practices like racial covenants and allowed Black residents to purchase homes in the neighborhood and integrate the schools. In 1960, Inglewood was 99 percent white. By 1980, five years after my parents purchased their store, that number would drop to 8 percent.

My father's store was called Marv's Liquor, and it was open from 8:30 A.M. to 11:00 P.M. every day. Since my father couldn't afford to hire employees, he asked my grandfather to move to Los Angeles from Korea and help out. While my father manned the register, my grandfather restocked shelves and kept an eye out for shoplifters. In between hospital shifts, my mother would bring them food and take over the register while they scarfed down their meal. Most of my dad's customers were Black and middle-class and worked at nearby aerospace companies like Hughes and McDonnell Douglas. Many became regulars and even friends. Within months, the store was bringing in almost double what it had made in the past.

But my parents were already thinking of selling. In the year that they owned the store, they were robbed three times. The first time, it was about ten minutes before closing time. A man in a ski mask came in and pointed a handgun at my father, demanding money from the cash register. Despite the mask, my dad recognized the man—he was a regular customer. My father emptied the register. There was less than $100 in the till because he had learned to hide any extra money in the back in case something like this happened. The robber got away, but my father wasn't hurt and they hadn't lost an enormous amount of money. Still, the experience shook him. Was it worth risking his life to continue owning the store?

He got his answer with the second attempted robbery. It was in the middle of the day, around 2:00 P.M. Two men who my father had never seen before came into the store and wandered through the aisles. They left without buying anything, then returned two more times to look around before leaving. My father was sure they were casing his store. He asked my grandfather to go to the parking lot and jot down the men's license plate number. The next thing my father heard was my grandfather screaming. He ran outside and saw my grandfather clutching his head, blood everywhere. He'd been pistol-whipped.

My grandfather was rushed to the hospital, where he was treated and released. Luckily, his skull hadn't been fractured, and he recovered from his physical injuries. But the psychological damage was done. My father put the store on the market, briefly hopeful when a fellow Korean immigrant expressed interest in buying the place. Any prospective deal fell through, though, when the man's loan officer told him he'd be crazy to buy the store because he'd be certain to get killed.

In the meantime, the store was robbed a third time. It was again the middle of the day, and my father was at the register, training a new employee, the son of the dry cleaner's next door. They were held up at gunpoint and ordered to empty the register. This time, the robber got away with $500. My father had theft insurance, so he was quickly reimbursed for his loss. Yet the fear and stress of the job had taken its toll on the family. I was an infant, and my mother was pregnant with my sister. She was working long hours at the hospital and helping out at the store, plus living in a tiny apartment with a father-in-law she frankly couldn't stand.

On top of that, she was terrified of being left a widow. She and my father fought constantly. Why couldn't he go back to school and get a safe, professional job? Why did he send money back to his brothers and sisters in Korea when they were struggling *here*, in the States?

My father describes what happened next as a miracle. A young cigarette salesman asked him if he was interested in selling the store. Absolutely, my father said. The salesman said he knew of an interested buyer and offered to broker a deal. And it worked. In 1977, the new owner successfully applied for an SBA loan for Black-owned businesses, and the store returned to Black ownership. My parents were able to recoup their initial investment and even made a profit. They used the money to buy their first house in nearby Rancho Park, a house that had a racial covenant attached to the deed, a house they could not have purchased ten years earlier because of their race.

I recently asked my father what race the robbers were. Black. What race were the owners of the dry cleaner's next door? Black. What race was the cigarette salesman? Black. My father had never interacted so closely with Black people before. And many of his customers had never interacted so closely with an Asian person before. A story begins to take shape as I put these words down on the page. Did you fall into the narrative groove of Black criminality and violence? Or did you fall into the groove of Asian foreignness and model minority-ness? Did you wonder if my dad was racist, or if his customers were racist? Did you begin to construct a story of Black-Asian conflict?

Hold up a second. Where were the white people during

all of this? They were in the suburbs, where they'd fled after Black people began moving into Inglewood. They were in the banks, approving my father's loan for a store in a neighborhood they'd never step foot in. They were in the courts, fighting efforts to desegregate LA public schools. They were everywhere and nowhere. The story of Black-Asian relations in this country is the story of whiteness, which set the stage for the drama to come. Whiteness cast Asians as perpetual foreigners and the model minority, cast Black people as perpetual criminals and the problem minority, then sat on the sidelines to watch what happened.

Left behind by white people but still shaped by the logic of white supremacy, my father and his Black customers were *supposed* to see each other as rivals rather than allies. They'd been trapped in the American racial imaginary, that sleight of hand that makes all of us focus on one another's differences rather than on the sharp white background of white supremacy. The forces that endorsed segregation, policed Black communities, and starved them of resources and opportunities are the same forces that deemed those of Asian descent "unfit" for American citizenship, banned them from immigrating to the United States, and incarcerated them in concentration camps during World War II. Whiteness maintains its power, and communities of color are left to fight for their place on the lower rungs of the American racial hierarchy.

I was only a child, but I was figuring out how the racial imaginary worked. Already, I could sense there was a racial hierarchy in the country and that I was *not* at the top— otherwise, why would I constantly have to explain "what" I was and reduce myself to a caricature? Yet instead of pondering—and questioning—*why* that was, I was being distracted. Misdirected. Don't look at the white. Look at the color. Look at nonwhite people the way white people look at you. Look at the Asian. Look at the Black.

* * *

When I was eight years old, Cabbage Patch Kids were all the rage. I generally hated dolls, much preferring the free stuffed animals my dad brought home from the now-defunct Crocker bank (charmingly called "Crocker spaniels"). But the white kids at school all had Cabbage Patch Kids, and I began to covet one, too. My parents could not afford one—they'd told me so—but in my diary that year, I nonetheless recorded my Christmas wish list:

Cabbage Patch doll with 한복
My own 한복 (including shoes)

In 1984, the only Asian Cabbage Patch Kid I'd ever seen was a Japanese one that was advertised on TV. It had black yarn hair cut in bangs and wore a red kimono. I knew I wasn't Japanese; I knew I wasn't Chinese; I wanted a Korean doll. Despite any proof that such a doll existed, I held out hope Santa/my parents would somehow magically produce a Korean Cabbage Patch Kid. On Christmas morning, I opened my gifts with giddy anticipation. As usual, I got a value-pack of Korean underwear and some Scholastic books, but there was still one misshapen package under the tree that I was *sure* was the doll. In a frenzy, I tore open the wrapping paper and discovered . . . a stuffed bunny. In my diary the next day, I documented my disappointment. All

I'd asked for was an "oriental" Cabbage Patch Kid. Why did I never, ever get what I wanted?

I routinely referred to myself as "oriental" at this age. My parents and I frequently used the term, with no sense that it might be pejorative or offensive. My uncle, my father's youngest brother, was studying oriental medicine. The supermarket had a small oriental food section. Federal legislation from the 1970s included the terms "Oriental" and "Negro." But as Edward Said argued in his 1978 book *Orientalism*, the "Orient" was a European confabulation, a colonial construct that lumped the "Middle East" (or Southwest Asia), East Asia, and South/Southeast Asia together in opposition to the West. "Orientals" were supposed to be exotic and foreign; they were the perpetual other; they were, by extension, subordinate and inferior. They could be mocked with slanty-eyed gestures, as I'd learned through the playground chant. In the eyes of America, I was indistinguishable from Chinese or Japanese—or Vietnamese or Thai or Filipino. According to this racial logic, I should be perfectly happy to have a Japanese Cabbage Patch Kid because in this country, we were all considered "oriental."

A month or so later, my father took me to a discount toy store in Inglewood that somehow had Cabbage Patch Kids in stock. He knew I'd been disappointed not to get a doll for Christmas and wanted to make it up to me. I tried to set my expectations as I entered the store, telling myself that I couldn't be picky and that I would be happy with *any* "oriental" doll. Scanning the shelves, I realized with a shock that all the Cabbage Patch Kids were Black. I scanned row after row for the Japanese doll, but it wasn't there. There were no white dolls, either. Every single doll was Black.

My dad grabbed one of the dolls off the shelf and said, "How about this one?" I shook my head. No way. "What about this one?" he asked, taking a different one off the shelf. No. My dad laughed. "You don't want *any* of these dolls?" He seemed amused. Cabbage Patch Kids were expensive, and it was a huge deal that my parents were willing to buy me one. But I was adamant—I'd rather go home empty-handed than have a Black doll.

The memory now fills me with horror, yet I recall with utter clarity my train of thought. If I couldn't have a Korean doll, I would be OK with a Japanese doll. If I couldn't have a Japanese doll, I would be OK with a white doll. But if there were no white dolls, I would rather have no doll at all. Those Black dolls at the store were a confirmation of the racial hierarchy I'd internalized. The Black dolls were "discount" dolls, the ones no one wanted, the ones that were still available and, thus, inferior. The desirable dolls were the white dolls, and they were all sold out. I did not want a second-class doll.

I was reminded of this experience years later when learning about Mamie and Kenneth Clark's famous doll experiment, which was cited as part of the landmark Supreme Court case *Brown v. Board of Education.* The Clarks were a husband-and-wife team of child psychologists who conducted a series of tests on Black children, asking them to choose between white and brown dolls based on questions ranging from "Give me the doll that you like to play with the best" and "Give me the doll that looks bad" to "Give me the doll that is a nice color" or "Give me the doll that looks like you." Most of the children attended segregated schools, and most demonstrated a preference for the white doll over the brown. Occasionally, if asked to point out which doll looked most like themselves, some children pointed to the brown doll and said "I'm a n—r." Others would refuse to answer the question, cry, or run out of the room.

The Clarks saw this as concrete evidence of the dehumanizing effects of segregation, which had so convinced the Black children of their own inferiority as to cause lasting psychological damage. White supremacist culture had taught these children to hate themselves, to correlate their skin color with negative traits and to internalize their own abjection. They, too, preferred the white dolls. As a child growing up in the 1980s, nearly forty years after the abolition of de jure segregation, I still implicitly understood that Black stood at the bottom rung of the American racial hierarchy. Faced with a choice between Black and white, I would always choose white.

Even more so than Barbies and other popular dolls, Cabbage Patch Kids invited—in fact *demanded*—personal identification. The dolls came with "adoption papers," and purchasing a doll was framed as an "adoption fee." Your Cabbage Patch Kid was your de facto adopted child, a mini-me, a double. In my diary entry, I clearly understood this—I wanted not only a Korean Cabbage Patch Kid wearing hanbok, but also my own set of hanbok so that we could match, the doll a perfect manifestation of my own ego. Yet staring at the shelves full of Black dolls, I understood that Black life (and even its uncanny surrogate, the Black doll) was less desirable. Cheaper—literally. To "adopt" one of these Black dolls was to identify with Blackness, and I reacted the way some of the children in the Clarks' experiment reacted: with racial panic. I did not want to be Black.

The fact that I clung to the dream of an "oriental" doll is no less distressing. I'd learned the art of racial concession to whiteness, accepting Japanese for Korean (my own grandfather would have lost his mind if he knew I had a "Japanese" doll). But I'd also accepted a "foreign" doll. No other Cabbage Patch Kid that I recall wore traditional clothing like a kimono—none of the white Cabbage Patch Kids, none of the Black Cabbage Patch Kids. Despite being born in the United States, I would always be cast as foreign. (I guess purchasing an Asian Cabbage Patch Kid meant I'd be participating in an international adoption.)

If someone had asked me which doll looked most like me, I would have pointed to the Japanese doll and said, "I'm oriental."

I would not have cried. I would not have run out of the room. I would have been grateful the white gaze had seen me at all.

Chapter Three

BAD ACTORS

From first to sixth grade, I attended a predominantly white Catholic school in West Los Angeles, where I was one of a handful of Asian students. Most of my classmates were Irish or Italian Catholic and generations removed from their immigrant forebears, having assimilated into a general fratty whiteness. The only other Asian girl in my class was biracial, with a white father and American-born Chinese mother. This girl and her mother studiously avoided my mother and me, as if to emphasize that while we shared some racial characteristics, we had little else in common. They had fully merged into white American culture. My mother and I, meanwhile, were still outsiders.

My first friend at that school was an Irish-Italian girl named Erin who was born prematurely and had a large scar on her arm, the result of an IV mishap when she was an infant. Erin lived with her mother near the school, in a duplex that smelled of cigarette smoke and had large, signed posters of *M*A*S*H* hanging on the wall. Erin's mother had been a script supervisor on the series, which ended its run in 1983, and she was on unemployment while trying to get staffed on a new show. I had never seen *M*A*S*H** but vaguely knew it was about the Korean War. My parents, who had actually lived through the war, had never seen an episode, either.

Erin's mother eventually landed a job on a new sitcom called *Designing Women*, another show that I did not watch. I was now ten years old, and my favorite sitcom was *Punky Brewster*. I watched the show every week with my dad and sister, rapt as Punky dealt with the aftermath of the *Challenger* disaster or learned the dangers of hiding in abandoned refrigerators. Though my family lived in LA, Erin's mom was the only person we knew who was in "The Industry." When she asked if my sister and I wanted to audition for a part in *Designing Women*, I was thrilled. I thought I was going to be the next Soleil Moon Frye.*

My mother, on the other hand, was dubious. She already thought TV was a bad influence, rotting my brain when I could be practicing the piano or doing my homework. She also believed actors were one step removed from prostitutes, parading themselves in front of strangers for money and attention. Erin's mom was persistent, though, telling her that the casting director was having trouble finding enough Asian child actors to audition for the role. She assured her that it would be a wholesome experience.

I'd never acted before, not even in a school play. In the car on the way to Warner Bros. Studio in Burbank, my sister and I rehearsed the audition script. The part was for a Vietnamese boat child named Li Sing, whom ex–beauty queen Suzanne Sugarbaker (Delta Burke) agrees to foster for a few weeks. I didn't know anyone Vietnamese and wondered if

---

* Fun fact: Soleil Moon Frye and I were born one day apart.

I was supposed to have an accent. I couldn't even imitate a Korean accent—I talked like a Valley girl. The scene took place in Suzanne's "powder room," where Li Sing played with the fancy bath products and bantered with Suzanne. "What's a powder room?" I asked my mom from the backseat. "I have no idea," she snapped. She was in a bad mood—Burbank was on the opposite end of the city, across four major freeways at the height of afternoon rush hour.

An hour later, we pulled into the studio lot, and the guard in the kiosk directed us to a bungalow. As we waited to be seen by the casting director, I saw another Asian girl in a party dress and frilly socks, holding a headshot in her hands. She looked like a pro, skipping into the casting room when called. Her mother eyed us while we waited. My sister and I did not have headshots. We'd come straight from school and were still wearing our plaid jumpers. My mother had on her Pioneer Chicken uniform of brown pants, a beige shirt, and SAS shoes. I kept my eyes down, trying to memorize the script, feeling increasingly nervous. A short time later, the girl bounced out, looking pleased and telling her mother she thought it went well.

It was now my turn. I was ushered into a small office where a white woman and white man greeted me, then seated themselves on director chairs. They asked for my headshot and I told them I didn't have one. No problem, they said. The woman explained it was a big role, with lots of screen time. In the episode, Li Sing and Suzanne would become fast friends, and Li Sing would even get to wear Suzanne's pageant tiara and dress like her, in big hair and makeup and a 1980s power suit. Uh-huh, I said. I'd seen a picture of Delta Burke and thought she looked like a member of Whitesnake.

The woman began running through the lines with me, playing Suzanne Sugarbaker to my Li Sing. It was over in a minute.

For days afterward, I pestered my mother—"Did I get it? Did I get it?" Eventually, Erin's mother broke the news, saying my sister and I "didn't look Vietnamese enough" and that the casting director had decided to go with a professional actor. I was crestfallen—so much for child stardom—but mixed in with my disappointment was a dawning awareness that my race itself required a kind of performance. I knew Li Sing was supposed to be a ham, like any other child actor in a sitcom. But I also understood I was supposed to perform a stereotypical Asian-ness, which meant speaking in broken English, marveling at American novelties like bubble bath and Southern belles, and becoming Suzanne's doll and plaything. Li Sing wasn't even a Vietnamese name.* She might as well have been called "Oriental Girl #1."†

I wish I could say I felt degraded by this realization, or angry at the white screenwriter for writing such a caricatured role. But I was mostly annoyed at the other Asian girl I'd seen at the audition, the one in the froufrou dress. I was certain she had landed the role and that she'd been able to give them the performance they wanted. *She* was my competition for white attention and approval, and she had won out.

* * *

By the time I started at my new all-girls school, I desperately wanted an Asian friend, preferably Korean. A Korean

---

* She may have been Vietnamese of ethnic Han Chinese ancestry, but her name would have been spelled Lê Sáng.
† For a brilliant parody of Hollywood's stereotypical Asian parts, read Charles Yu's *Interior Chinatown*.

friend would get me in a way my white friends like Erin could not; we could complain to each other about our parents, fangirl over Carrie Ann Inaba on *In Living Color*, and make mixtapes on my Panasonic boom box. My new school was predominantly white, but there was a sizeable minority of Asian American students, especially Korean Americans. The campus abutted Koreatown, and some wealthier Korean families had moved into the neighborhood and started sending their daughters to the school. With its all-girls student body, conservative culture, and academic reputation, the school was particularly attractive to these parents, many of whom had graduated from prominent, single-sex high schools and universities back home. For the first time, I was attending school with a significant number of Asian American girls, and not just the children of working-class shopkeepers like my parents, but the children of doctors, businessmen, and other professionals.

At first, I thought my dreams had been answered. I met a Korean American girl named Hannah, whose parents owned a dry cleaner's in Cerritos. While Hannah's dad manned the store, her mom made the hour-plus commute to school in their station wagon every morning and parked outside, waiting *seven hours* until school ended so she could ferry Hannah back home. I thought this was crazy, but my mother held an awed respect for the lengths Hannah's parents went to for their daughter's education.

Hannah was not an angry little Asian girl. She was very close to her parents and unfailingly obedient. Unlike me, she was raised in a Korean community, attended Korean church, and socialized with Koreans. She was also fluent in Korean and was horrified when she discovered how little Korean

I knew. I'd always resisted speaking Korean at home and attending Korean language school, desperate to assimilate into my white American school and neighborhood. Now I found myself being accused of being too Americanized, too white, not Korean enough.

I couldn't understand why Hannah wasn't angry. She respected her parents, appreciated their sacrifices for her, and didn't find them overly protective. She thought Korean culture and values were superior. She excelled in math and science, planning to become a doctor, like her parents wanted. And she never wavered or rebelled, even as she grew older. She graduated a year early from high school after being admitted to an accelerated medical program in the Midwest. Her parents moved with her across the country. Thirty years later, Hannah is now a doctor at a prestigious medical center, married to another Korean doctor, and the mother of twin boys. Her parents live with her and help take care of her children.

Hannah fit the mold of the model minority. Most of her friends were Korean or East Asian, and she dutifully stayed in her racial lane. Even the white girls liked her, squealing over her as if she were a doll or a pet. In eighth grade, she ran for treasurer of our class with a slogan taken from the 1980s Nuprin commercial: "Little. Yellow. Different. Better." She won.

I envied Hannah. Maybe she was brainwashed, but I longed to be that content, to be accepted within the Korean community while also being accepted within the larger white American one. I didn't know why I couldn't be the same, navigating these worlds with the ease and success of Hannah.

Most of my close friends during the time were East, Southeast, and South Asian, all of them the daughters of immigrants.* Some had white-collar professionals as parents and some had parents like mine, small business owner-operators of liquor stores, dry cleaner's, grocery stores. We studied together, went to the mall together, bumped into each other at supermarkets or hagwons in Koreatown. We were academically driven, with parents who expected us to excel and to eventually attend "good" colleges.

Outside of this small group were other Asian Americans whom we rejected as either "too white" or "too Asian," as if we were playing a game of Goldilocks and we were the only ones who were just right. There were a few East Asian and South Asian girls who ran in entirely white crowds. They were generally not friends with each other (there was only room for one Asian person in each white clique), but they shared economically privileged backgrounds, with doctor parents and fancy homes in the neighborhood. My father would often ask me why I wasn't close to Esther, whose dad was a prominent radiologist in Koreatown. "Because I'm Korean," I said, "and Esther hates Korean people." At school, my friends and I called girls like Esther whitewashed and complained to one another, "It's like they don't even know they're Asian."

Of course, I'd been called whitewashed, too, and a bad Korean—by Hannah. I retaliated by deeming people like her too Asian. As I got older, I found her unquestioning absorption of Korean cultural values a sign of intellectual

---

* I was also friends with other non-Asian POC (my class had a small number of Black students and an even smaller number of Latinx students), but the vast majority of nonwhite students at my school were Asian American, and I want to focus on them here.

weakness. Her family was devoutly Christian, and she once told a Jewish classmate that she was going to hell. She spoke denigratingly of Black people. She thought homosexuality was a sin. According to her, mixed-race kids were unnatural and impure. Behind her back, I used to mock her for her dorky Korean socks, with their off-brand logo and ankle fit. Every Christmas, I got the same socks and also underwear, either mailed to me from Korean relatives or purchased from the local swap meet. I saw them as a further sign of my difference, my own off-brand-ness, and so I refused to wear them.

There were other Asian girls I deemed too Asian as well, and by that, I meant that they made "us" look bad by being so stereotypically nerdy, fulfilling the model minority trope. There was Stephanie, the daughter of Taiwanese immigrants, who wore Coke bottle glasses and carried a Sanrio pencil box filled with mechanical pencils. She dressed in hopelessly too-long skirts and had greasy black hair that she pulled back with a satin headband. In class, she always sat in the front row and filled her notebooks with her impeccable handwriting. I reserved a special disdain for these girls. Among my friends, we sneered at how nerdy they were, what losers they were. We ignored them in the halls, just as the whitewashed Asian girls ignored us.

In retrospect, I'm appalled at how thoroughly my thinking had been distorted by the experience of being a minoritized person in a predominantly white space. A few years ago, while following *Crazy Rich Asians* author Kevin Kwan on Twitter, I felt a shock of recognition at how Kwan described moving to Texas from Singapore in the 1980s. The meanest kids weren't the white kids—it was the Asian

American kids. For them, the appearance of Kevin, with his foreign accent and his uncool clothes, elicited disgust and even fear. Here was this FOB making the cool, American-born, assimilated Asian kids look bad. How precarious was their acceptance into American society that one Asian immigrant could immediately cast the whole teenage Asian American community into the shadow of foreignness and difference!

I reserved a special kind of anger for these "too white" and "too Asian/FOBby" classmates. It was the flame of self-hatred. What I hated in them was what I hated the most in myself—their too-successful efforts to assimilate into whiteness, or their not-successful-enough efforts to escape from their Asian-ness. By focusing on their perceived flaws, I didn't have to confront my own. *At least I'm not as white-washed as* they *are*, I told myself. Or *At least I'm not as FOBby as* they *are*.

Yet where I situated myself was no less distorted by white supremacist culture than where I situated other Asian Americans. I was contorting myself into a category of "just rightness," framed by and defined by whiteness. Even in this space, I could not escape anger or self-hatred. Was I acting and behaving too white? Or acting and behaving too Asian? Was I also a racial grotesque? Was my love of literature and writing a reaction to racist assumptions that Asians were good at math? What was authentic about my identity, and what had been warped by my environment?

I often think about a former classmate, Priya, who graduated near the top of our class. We remained in the same social group through junior high and high school. Priya had shortened her long "ethnic" last name to make it easier for Americans to pronounce. She was extraordinarily smart, self-deprecating, and witty. She made fun of her lack of athletic and artistic ability. She was terrified of her skin getting too dark in the sun, covering herself in what looked like a hazmat suit when we spent a week hiking outdoors for a class field trip. Once, she was cleaning chalkboard erasers with us after math class and held up her brown hand, now covered in white chalk dust. "Look!" she said. "I'm finally white, the color I've always wanted to be!"

Those of us who were there (all women of color) reacted in horror, and Priya responded by saying it was just a joke. But she coveted whiteness, worshipped it, abjected herself to it. Though she stayed within our predominantly Asian social group, she made herself an ad hoc mascot to the white girls in class. She never presumed to join their parties or social activities (her parents were extremely strict, and she was never allowed out of her house). But she pandered to whiteness, made herself the butt of jokes—usually about how ugly, awkward, and nerdy she was—and found acceptance in their laughter.

I had never seen anything like it. In fact, I still have never seen anything like it. It was only much later, when I was doing research on blackface minstrelsy, that I finally found a lens to understand Priya's behavior. She had turned herself into a racial grotesque, a comic avatar of Asian-ness. In exaggerating and performing racial stereotypes of the model minority, she courted the affection of the white majority. "We love you, Priya!" was the common refrain from white classmates. "You're so funny!" and "Oh my God, stop saying you're so uncool! You're awesome!" By demeaning herself, by rendering herself a clown and a fool, Priya was contorting herself into a *funny* little Asian girl.

People like Hannah had also been adopted as "pets" by the white majority, accepted in certain spaces (school) and not others (home, parties). They were unthreatening and adorable. But Priya's performance went further by leveraging laughter in the service of white acceptance. Like a brownface (yellowface?) minstrel, she practiced a form of shucking and jiving, a performative racial buffoonery. When her audience laughed, it served as a balm to her feelings of racial self-hatred. They were laughing *with* her, right? Not *at* her?

Rereading the previous paragraphs, I'm shocked by my raw anger at Priya. *Clown. Fool. Shucking and jiving.* These are terrible, wounding words. Words that Mrs. Church would have deemed overly harsh and inflammatory. Too full of rage and too racialized.

And yet, these are the same words that I have lodged against myself and others have lodged against me. Sellout. Twinkie. Fool. Toward Priya I feel a rage and disgust rooted in self-hatred and self-recognition. I, too, have practiced a kind of frantic, humiliating dance to be accepted in the white world. I, too, have achieved some measure of mainstream white acceptance—Ivy League degrees, a comfortable life-style, a job in the ivory tower. I see myself in Priya, and I hate what I see.

Chapter Four

THE FORGOTTEN WAR

My father met an American for the first time during the Korean War. He was nine or ten years old, and his family had fled from the North to the South just before the border shut down. They'd stayed briefly at a refugee camp and then made their way to a relative's house farther south. There was no food. My father's mother would gather weeds from the surrounding fields and boil it for soup. The only people who had enough to eat were the American GIs, so children would beg soldiers for castoff rations—tins of Spam, chocolate, cigarettes.

My dad was one of these starving kids. He was warned to stay away from American soldiers, but one day, as he was walking down the street, a Black serviceman gestured at him to come over. My father was scared. He had never seen a Black person up close, and he couldn't understand what this soldier wanted with him. The GI pulled a colorful object from his pocket and mimed the act of eating. He gave the object to my father, along with an encouraging smile. An older neighbor, who had witnessed the entire exchange, cornered my father afterward. "Throw it away," he instructed.

"It's probably poison." My father complied. Even though he was starving, he threw out the GI's gift. Decades later, my father would recognize the colorful object at a liquor store in Philadelphia. It was a roll of Life Savers.

This story broke my heart as a kid. My poor, starving father. The kind, benevolent GI. To this day, you can see the legacy of malnutrition in my father's oversize head, his short stature, his bowed legs. You can also see it in his inability to say no whenever my sister and I complained that we were hungry. Every time we passed a McDonald's, we would beg for a Happy Meal, and nine times out of ten, he would stop to get it for us. It drove my mom crazy. He can't stand it when our dog begs for food, either, sneaking her table scraps and extra scoops of kibble when he thinks we aren't looking.

Now that I'm older, though, I'm not so sure how to feel about the encounter. "Don't take candy from strangers." How many times had I heard that growing up? Also, "There's no such thing as a free lunch." American soldiers often handed out candy to kids in war zones. It was an ingenious form of ideological grooming. Ingratiate yourself to the local population by dispensing sweets, like some kind of fairy godmother of democracy. Make them associate you with food and wealth and kindness, instead of violence, fear, and deprivation. Make them see America as the benevolent savior.

My father threw out the candy, but he never stopped seeing America as synonymous with opportunity. His fear of the soldier was a fear of the other, but it was mixed with curiosity and desire. I wonder what the soldier thought. He probably saw a starving kid and felt bad for him. He was an American soldier, likely serving in a segregated unit.* What would he think if he knew my father would eventually immigrate to America and open up a liquor store, selling Life Savers to customers like him?

* * *

My father is slow to anger, something I attribute to his almost superhuman ability to endure physical and psychological pain. Rather than complain about a broken hip (or burst appendix or second-degree burns all over his body), he sucks it up. I used to assume this was part of his cultural conditioning—chae-myun—but as I got older, I realized it was a survival tactic honed over years of unimaginable suffering. As a child, my father lived through Japanese colonialism, war, famine, poverty, and displacement. He learned to absorb humiliations large and small, to demonstrate forbearance rather than anger when disciplined by his father, or terrorized by North Korean sentries, or mocked for his poverty by his classmates and teachers. Recently, my father admitted to me that he had an "inferiority complex," a phrase that surprised me, given his general disinclination to self-reflection. But it makes sense. My father doesn't complain because after years of being treated like garbage, he's internalized his own worthlessness.

My father was born in Japan-occupied Korea in 1938, when his mother was twenty years old and his father

---

* In 1948, President Truman issued an executive order desegregating the armed forces. The Army resisted integration, and Congressman Charles Rangel, who served with distinction in the Korean War, recalls that in 1950, desegregation "did not get down to the troops at all." It was only after President Eisenhower fired General MacArthur in 1951 and the Army sustained major combat losses that desegregation of units truly began in earnest.

twenty-five. He was their firstborn and, for the next five years, their only child. Shortly after his birth, his family moved to Pyongyang, in the north. Under Japanese rule, Koreans were brutally repressed and plundered of their culture, land, and labor. The Japanese forbade the teaching of Korean language and history, forced Korean women into sexual slavery, and conscripted Korean men to work in Japanese factories and mines. My father and his family were required to speak Japanese and to take Japanese names. Employed by the postal service, my grandfather made so little money that my grandmother worked as an illegal street vendor, selling sweet potatoes that she bought from local farmers and roasted at home. She was arrested several times by the Japanese police, resulting in heavy fines that left her with no choice but to keep selling potatoes to pay them off.

In 1945, when my father was six, the Allied forces liberated Korea from Japan, ending thirty-five years of colonial rule and ushering in a new period of foreign occupation. Korea became Solomon's baby, split in half at the 38th parallel by the Soviet Union and the United States. The Soviet army moved into Pyongyang to drive out the remaining Japanese soldiers and civilians. They were a shabby lot, inadequately dressed for the brutally cold winter in their ragged uniforms. Under their arms, they had tucked loaves of hard black bread, which they would tear pieces from to eat during the day and then use as pillows at night. Many were Russian farm boys, uneducated and provincial, and they marveled at the modern contraptions owned by Korean people. Marching up to civilians, they'd strip them of their watches and fountain pens at gunpoint and then parade around with their loot, five watches to a wrist, fountain pens bristling from their pockets.

For a brief period after liberation, my father's family enjoyed prosperity catering to these raggedy Russian soldiers. My grandmother could do some basic sewing, so my grandfather bought leather on the black market and my grandmother stitched it into coats to sell. The results were laughable, but no matter how crooked the seams were, how ill-fitting or janky, the soldiers couldn't get enough of them. They had plenty of rapidly depreciating military currency to spend, and they spent it like drunken sailors. With the money they made, my grandparents moved into a house that had been abandoned by a Japanese family. It was the nicest home they'd ever lived in, with an indoor toilet and a magical hand-crank phonograph that played music.

But my grandfather was getting worried. As the Soviets withdrew and Kim Il Sung consolidated power, my grandfather watched as the new regime began cracking down on dissent and imposing new restrictions on travel and commerce. On a trip south to visit relatives, he was unexpectedly arrested, detained, and beaten by North Korean border guards, an experience that only convinced him that the family had to flee *now*, before the border completely shut down. My grandmother balked, reluctant to give up a life of comparative comfort for the insecure life of a refugee. My grandfather threatened to leave and take my father with him, abandoning her with their younger son, now a toddler. She caved.

They sold everything at a steep loss and took a train to the border city of Haeju, on the western coast of the peninsula facing the Yellow Sea. The border was now virtually impass-able, and the station was full of fellow refugees desperate to make it to the South. Using the last of his money, my grandfather hired a guide and two young men to smuggle them across the border, one man carrying my father on his back, the other carrying his brother. They waited until nightfall with a group of ten to fifteen migrants, watching the guide collect his money and then motion them into the darkness.

My father must have fallen asleep while being carried on the smuggler's back because the next thing he remembers is being jolted awake by a volley of gunshots and shouts of "Freeze!" and "Don't move or we'll shoot you!" In the chaos that followed, the smugglers took off into the darkness. The rest of the group was rounded up by North Korean border guards and thrown into jail. As they were being herded into a holding cell, the guards recognized my grandfather from his previous arrest. Yanking him out of line, they drew their guns and threatened to shoot him on the spot. In the end, they spared his life but beat him senseless.

The guards released my grandmother and her children, but they continued to hold my grandfather captive. The family was now completely destitute, with nowhere to go—no money for train fare back to Pyongyang, no home there to return to, anyway. My grandmother begged an elderly local farmer to take them in, and for days she kept vigil by the window, her eyes fixed on the main road for any sign of her husband. When he finally appeared one day, a forlorn figure trudging down the dirt road, my grandmother was so overcome with relief that she ran out of the house barefoot.

Her elation didn't last long. "We have to cross again immediately," my grandfather said. "There's no time." The farmer told them that it was safest to cross in the evening, while the guards were eating dinner. That evening, as soon as they saw smoke coming from the dining barracks, they followed the farmer to an opening in a grassy field. They crossed alone this time, with no guide, no men to carry the children, no fellow refugees. My grandfather carried my father on his back, my grandmother carried my uncle on hers. In the summer dusk, they crept through the waist-high grass, stooping to conceal themselves, terrified that my uncle would cry and give them away.

Darkness fell. No one stopped them. As the minutes passed, my father relaxed a little. Maybe they were going to make it, after all. But just as he was about to doze off, he felt my grandfather stop abruptly in his tracks. Instantly, my father was awake and alert. Directly ahead of them was a sea of flashlights. My father felt a rush of cold fear come over his body. It was all over—they'd walked squarely into a border patrol. For several excruciating moments, they waited to be discovered. The lights bobbed up and down, came closer. My father prepared to die.

Yet human voices never materialized in the darkness. The lights continued to blink, but no soldier emerged to arrest them. After what felt like an interminable amount of time, my grandfather crept forward. The lights now surrounded them, flickering and dancing. My father had never seen such a thing before.

"What are they?" he asked, gazing at the lights in awe.

"Fireflies," my grandfather answered.

They walked for another couple of miles, unsure where North Korea ended and South Korea began. At some point, they hit a road and heard a man whistling. When the man caught sight of them, they backed away in fear, but he reassured them, "Don't worry, you're safe. You're in the South." He pointed them in the direction of a refugee camp, where they joined countless other families who had fled the North. The camp officials hosed them down with a chemical disinfectant, gave them a small amount of money, and released them a few days later. With the money, they bought train tickets and headed to Nonsan, where my grandfather's brother lived.

* * *

Every Korean person of a certain age has memories of the fear, hunger, and suffering during the period around the Korean War. Over the years, I've managed to pry bits and pieces from my parents, but their memories are fragmented and incomplete. They don't want to talk about it, and they especially don't want to talk about it in English, which is foreign and clumsy and insufficient. Even my attempts to transcribe my father's story above feel forced, overdramatized. My parents passed down their memories of war in nonverbal ways, in the hoarding of plastic bags and the aversion to waste, in the fear of authority and a general low-level paranoia. Be ready to flee. Be prepared to lose everything. Don't trust anyone.

To Americans, the Korean War is the forgotten war, wedged chronologically between World War II and Vietnam. Even its start date and end date are blurry. When North Korea invaded the South in June 1950, President Truman deployed American troops to the region without securing congressional approval to declare war. Three years later, North Korea, China, and the United States signed an armistice agreement to end the fighting. South Korea never signed, refusing to accept the division of its country. In other words, the war never officially began, and it never officially ended. Technically, the country is still at war.

For Koreans, the war isn't forgotten—it's seared into the collective memory of the country. Three million people died in the conflict, the vast majority of them civilians. Why do you think so many of us immigrated to this country? We are here because America was there. Today, South Korea has remade itself into an economic powerhouse, but in the years after the war, it was what Trump would call a shithole country. In addition to the bombed-out landscape, the disease, the hunger, and the masses of refugees, this was a country literally divided in half at the 38th parallel. When people ask me if my family immigrated here from North or South Korea, I want to laugh. I wouldn't be here if my parents had been living in North Korea. No one gets out of North Korea unless they defect or they're Dennis Rodman. The only Koreans in America are South Koreans.

And what does that even mean? Korea is Korea. The designations "North" and "South" are man-made, the boundary imaginary while also strenuously enforced. Families were severed from one another—parents separated from children, husbands from wives, brother from brother. That's a wound that doesn't heal. Relatives became ghosts—dead but not dead, a phantom pain that never goes away. My parents both left Korea around 1970, when the memory of war was still fresh and the country was emerging from a period of postwar deprivation and political instability. Add to this the stress of immigration, of racism, of language acquisition, of economic precarity, of culture shock, and I wonder how my parents survived at all.

If you're Korean and you've read this far, you're probably wondering when I'm going to talk about han. Among my friends, it captures something quintessential about the Korean character. There's no equivalent term in English, but I've heard it variously described as a condition of sorrow, bitterness, resentment, vengeance, and rage. Some have traced it to Korea's history of constant invasion and subjugation by more powerful neighbors like Japan. Others have associated it with the trauma of family separation and a divided country after the Korean War. Passed down from generation to generation, han is a bitter patrimony, an inheritance of loss.

I first learned of han through my grad school classmate Seo-Young Chu, whose own family tragically lost several members during the Korean War. Seo-Young argued that second-generation Korean Americans like us also experienced han. Though we did not personally experience the trauma of Japanese colonization or the Korean War, our parents and grandparents had transmitted that historical memory to us. We, too, were haunted by the collective grief of our ancestors.*

When Seo-Young described han to me, my first thought was *holy shit*. How had I not known about han before? It so accurately captured the combination of shame, melancholy, and rage that I thought uniquely individual to me. I will hold on to a grudge forever. I experience spectacular schaden-

---

* See Seo-Young Chu, "Science Fiction and Postmemory *Han* in Contemporary Korean American Literature."

freude. I sometimes think I will stroke out from rage. Maybe this was my cultural and genetic inheritance. I'd inherited the shadow of trauma—my depression, anxiety, and self-loathing were historical coping mechanisms. They'd ensured (and sometimes sabotaged) my ancestors' survival, and perhaps they would ensure or sabotage mine.

At the same time, I was wary of cultural essentialism. I hadn't even known what han was until I was twenty-five. Saying that Korean people suffered from han was like saying Irish people were innately mournful and funny and hard-drinking because they'd been brutally oppressed by the English for centuries.* While there may be some truth to these generalizations, they also tread uncomfortably close to stereotypes. The character of an entire people is reduced to its victimization at the hands of more powerful groups.

That being said, I believe han is real. And I know it's real for other Korean Americans—from scholars like Seo-Young Chu and Elaine Kim, who explored han in the aftermath of the 1992 LA Uprising, to the celebrity chef Dave Chang of Momofuku fame, who sees in his rage and his tortured relationship to his Korean heritage a manifestation of his own han. Korean people are vengeful and aggrieved and suffer from an inferiority complex (I can say this because I'm Korean). We repress our anguish so that it rots us from the inside out. We *never* get the chance to see the powerful and venal brought to justice, so when God and/or the universe and/or luck bring down the mighty, we don't feel bad. We feel a sick joy.

---

* Actually, Jay Caspian Kang writes that "Korean crazy" is "really just the same as Irish crazy, because both peoples come from small countries oppressed for hundreds of years by assholes across the way."

Korean women in particular can suffer from a specific type of han called hwa-byung, or "anger/fire disease." As Seo-Young writes, "Someone who dies of *han* is said to have died of *hwa-byung*" in a kind of spontaneous human combustion. To use the language of modern psychology, hwa-byung is considered a "culture-bound syndrome" or "cultural concept of distress."* Typically seen in middle-aged Korean women of low socioeconomic status, its symptoms include rage, insomnia, depression, heart palpitations, heavy sighing, a rising heat in the body, and stomach problems. Some researchers attribute it to the accumulated resentment and sense of injustice suffered by Korean women trapped in a patriarchal social system. If han is the curse of being Korean, hwa-byung is the curse of being Korean *and* a woman.

Thinking back, I realize my mother's jagged temper, her unpredictable violence, her fits of despair could not be reduced to anxiety, depression, or menopause, those inadequate diagnoses of Western medicine. They were symptoms of something more—a toxic cocktail of stressors like racism, patriarchy, economic precarity, and historical trauma. Han. My mother had repressed her anger, smoothing out her face in public, hiding behind the mask. But the anger was metastasizing, turning uncontrollable. While my sister responded by making herself smaller and quieter, I reacted with a growing fury of my own. I, too, felt powerless and persecuted, torn apart by an unspeak-

---

* The term "culture-bound syndrome" is controversial because it once again centers whiteness and implies that biological symptoms in non-Western groups can be attributed to cultural factors. In the *DSM-V*, "culture-bound syndrome" is renamed "cultural concept of distress."

able rage. The more I hated my mother, the more I found myself turning into her.

* * *

When I was nine years old, my dad walked out. My parents had been fighting constantly, and I would sometimes hear them screaming at each other at nighttime when I was supposed to be asleep. In one diary entry from this period, I described my father throwing a chair at my mother. The next day, my mother disappeared for several hours. My dad wanted to quit his job at Pacific Bell, where he'd worked as a clerk after selling the liquor store. It was a safe job with a steady paycheck, but my dad was aware he'd never rise in the company. That was the first time I heard him use the term "glass ceiling." He didn't have a college degree, his English was imperfect, and he was Asian. He wanted to buy another business—not a liquor store but maybe a motel in Riverside, or a fast-food restaurant. My mom was adamantly opposed.

One day, my father didn't come home. My mom discovered that their bank accounts had been frozen, and she panicked. No money, no husband, no explanation. When she finally tracked my dad down at work, he told her he wanted a divorce and that he would take me (I was his favorite) and she could keep my sister.

If I'd known this offer was on the table, I would have jumped at the chance to go with my dad. I secretly *wanted* them to get divorced because my dad didn't make us practice piano, didn't limit our television viewing, and bought us an Atari game console so we could play Pac-Man. Every night my sister and I would cry, asking when he was coming home. But for my mother, divorce was unthinkable. Korean people did not get divorced. The cultural stigma was so intense that my classmate Hannah wasn't allowed to visit our friend's apartment because the mother had divorced and remarried. My mother surrendered, informing my dad that he could do whatever he wanted so long as the family stayed together.

My father came home a few days later, quit his job, and spent the next year unemployed and looking for a new business while my mother supported the family. He would sit on the living room floor in his undershirt, newspapers spread all around him, classified ads circled in pen. On weekends, we spent hours on the freeway, looking at prospective businesses in the Inland Empire and South Bay. The motels were owned by South Asian immigrants. The fast-food businesses were owned by South or East Asian immigrants. My sister and I sat in the car, bored out of our minds as my parents talked to brokers. The fighting continued. "You must *never* depend on a man," my mother used to tell me. "Always have your own job, and your own money."

In 1986, my father bought a Pioneer Chicken franchise in Hawthorne, a neighborhood just south of Inglewood. Pioneer wasn't as cool as McDonald's, it wasn't even as cool as KFC, but at least we'd seen the commercials on TV starring O. J. Simpson ("The taste America loves best, Pioneeeeeer!"). My mom quit her job to help my dad, and we began to spend hours hanging out at the store while they worked. At first, my sister and I found the experience thrilling. We loved the bright orange fried chicken, the french fries, the soda fountain with dispensers for Orange and

Strawberry Bang. We'd push through the swinging door into the kitchen, where the floors were so greasy that we could skate around in our sneakers. In the back was a small office/supply room with sacks of batter mix, paper goods, and large carbon dioxide canisters for fountain drinks. We'd spin on the office chair, try on the paper hats that made us look like 1950s soda jerks, and mess around with my father's paper tape calculator. Once or twice a week, a truck would pull up to the back door and deliver large flats of chicken parts. The smell was overpowering—wet cardboard mixed with an animal tang. We'd avoid the walk-in fridge because it smelled to us like a morgue.

At home, we would help my father roll coins from the cash register into paper tubes so he could deposit them at the bank. He'd dump the coins out of burlap sacks and onto the carpet, where we would sit cross-legged and make little log piles that my dad then rubber-banded together. I loved the smell of coins and the sound they made when my mom cracked a tube open against the register drawer. I loved the Buffalo nickels and JFK half dollars and Susan B. Anthony dollars that would occasionally turn up. Sometimes my dad would show us counterfeit bills that were passed at the store—twenty-dollar bills that felt funny to the touch, or had the wrong tint, or had blurry details. He'd save two-dollar bills to show us, too, telling us that even though they looked fake, they were real.

The novelty wore off quickly. My parents worked every single day except Thanksgiving and Christmas. They wore identical uniforms—beige collared shirts, brown polyester pants, and striped clip-on ties in a garish orange, brown, and yellow. The shirts became threadbare, practically see-through, and no matter how much we washed them, they always smelled of stale grease. My sister and I got tired of eating restaurant castoffs for breakfast, lunch, and dinner—stale biscuits, limp chicken fingers, congealed mashed potatoes. Even dessert lost its appeal when my mother brought home expired cups of Boston cream pie and strawberry shortcake, with whipped cream topping that looked and tasted like wax.

A year or so after my parents bought the store, they hired a white woman to work as a cashier. They *never* hired white people, because white people generally did not apply for the crummy minimum-wage jobs that immigrants and Black and brown people usually filled in Los Angeles. But this woman was in her thirties, had work experience, and seemed responsible. They decided to take a chance. On weekends, my sister and I would spend time at the store, sitting at a table next to a bank of plastic ferns. The woman, let's say her name was Donna, would lean over the ferns and chat with us when business was slow. She had permed blond hair and reminded me of my teachers at school—she seemed so *American*, with her perfect English and her friendliness. Once she gave us foil-covered chocolate coins—gelt—and jokingly said they were real coins before peeling off the shell and laughing at our surprise. We loved her.

One day Donna cleaned out the cash register and took off. Then, to add insult to injury, she showed up a week later to pick up her paycheck. My mother refused, but Donna wouldn't leave without her money. They got into a screaming fight and my mother called the cops. Donna said she hadn't stolen anything; my mom said Donna was lying; the cops said my mom should just give Donna her paycheck and be grateful she hadn't lost more money. I felt sick at the betrayal. Donna had seemed so nice; all of us had been seduced by her. She'd given us candy, gained our confidence, and she'd stabbed us in the back. You can't trust anyone, my mom said.

The longer my mother worked at Pioneer, the more she saw the world as full of enemies—employees who cheated, customers who lied, robbers who stole, husbands who walked out, children who rebelled. Nobody could be trusted; everyone was out to get her. In 1988, Pioneer Chicken's corporate parent declared bankruptcy. A new owner took over the company and ran it further into the ground. In 1991, the company went bankrupt a second time. Franchise owners—many of them immigrants who had sunk their life savings into their store—were facing financial ruin. My parents had trouble paying rent, meeting payroll, and paying for my tuition. At home, my mother complained incessantly of stomach pain. Diagnosed with ulcers, she dwindled to ninety pounds. Every night, she would lie facedown on the floor, moaning and burping as my sister and I kneaded the knots out of her back.

By the time I entered high school, the model minority veneer I'd been trained to maintain had begun to crack. I was still doing well academically, but the rage I'd first put into words in my English class was now poisoning my daily interactions with teachers and classmates. I saw injustice everywhere; I felt powerless to change my situation. I was constantly being told I had a bad attitude.

Increasingly, the only person I *could* direct my rage toward was my mother, the person I saw as the apotheosis of everything oppressive. *She* was the one who screamed at me and threw shit at me. She was the one who pressured me to get good grades, forced me to go to a snooty private school, and saddled me with the responsibility of making all her misery worthwhile. My friend Eileen once came to pick me up from home, and as I left, my mother said something to me like "Be careful." I screamed back "Fuck you!" and slammed the door shut. "She's such a fucking bitch," I complained to Eileen, rolling my eyes. Eileen was aghast. She also had a psycho Korean mom, and her ass would have been grass if she'd ever cursed her mom out, *period*, much less in front of a friend. I was terrified of my mom, but I was also so angry and depressed that I didn't care. I wanted my mom to hit me. I wanted to beat myself up.

As far as my mother was concerned, there were only two roads in front of me. One was the path of the model minority, pushed by white supremacy and propagated by Korean-language newspapers in their gushing profiles of straight-A, 1600 SATs, Westinghouse-winning, Harvard-bound children.* My mom would clip the articles out and post them on our fridge—these Korean overachievers from Asian enclaves like Rowland Heights and Cerritos, displayed next to pictures of Jesus and Pope John Paul II. The other was the path of delinquency and crime, gangbanging

---

* My friend Riva was literally one of these kids. She was featured in the *USA Today* Top Ten High School Kids issue, something that we still tease her about mercilessly.

and drugs. The papers were full of those stories, too, of unsupervised Korean kids going "wrong," joining gangs, and ending up in juvie/jail or dead. My mother was terrified I'd end up on the second path; she saw any sign of insubordination as proof I'd been led astray.

My mother didn't realize that I was on a third path: self-immolation. My anger-disease, my hwa-byung, was merging with the noxious anger I felt at my marginalization, my invisibility, my powerlessness. I wanted to light it all on fire, burn it all to the ground. And I was not alone. My city was about to explode.

Chapter Five

UNSPEAKABLE THINGS UNSPOKEN

> We live in a land where the past is always erased and America is the innocent future in which immigrants can come and start over, where the slate is clean. The past is absent or it's romanticized. This culture doesn't encourage dwelling on, let alone coming to terms with, the truth about the past.*
>
> —Toni Morrison

When I was fifteen years old, Los Angeles experienced one of the worst racial uprisings in this nation's history. On April 29, 1992, a jury acquitted four white police officers in the vicious beating of Rodney King, a Black motorist whose assault was captured on videotape. Over the next several days, the city exploded into violence, looting, and arson. Mayor Tom Bradley declared a state of emergency. Governor Pete Wilson deployed the National Guard. President George H. W. Bush sent in federal troops. By the

---

* From a conversation with Paul Gilroy, published in *Small Acts: Thoughts on the Politics of Black Cultures.*

end of the unrest, sixty-three people were dead, more than two thousand injured, and property damage was estimated to exceed one billion dollars.

That's one story about the LA Uprising. But there's another. This one involves a Korean liquor store owner, Soon Ja Du, who falsely accused a fifteen-year-old Black girl, Latasha Harlins, of shoplifting a $1.79 bottle of orange juice. After a physical scuffle, Harlins turned to leave, and Du shot her in the back of the head, killing her instantly. On November 15, 1991, a jury found Du guilty of voluntary manslaughter and recommended the maximum sentence of sixteen years in prison. Instead, trial judge Joyce Karlin suspended the sentence and placed Du under probation for five years, ordering her to perform four hundred hours of community service and pay a small fine. Du received no prison time.

Latasha Harlins's death was one of the catalysts of the 1992 LA Uprising, exposing the frayed relationship between Black residents and Korean merchants in South Los Angeles. Thousands of Korean-owned businesses were looted and torched. Deserted by the LAPD, Korean merchants armed themselves against looters, patrolling their businesses in the streets and from the roofs. They took to the radio waves, calling into local Korean-language station Radio Korea to plead for help from the community. Edward Song Lee, an eighteen-year-old Korean American whose parents worked at a swap meet, rushed to Koreatown to help. He was accidentally shot and killed by a Korean merchant who mistook him for a looter. The next day, his mother saw a black-and-white photograph in the *Korea Times* of her son, sprawled on his back on the ground, wearing a black shirt. *It can't be him*, she told herself. Eddie was wearing a white T-shirt when he left the house. Later, she would realize his T-shirt was black with blood.

The day after the Rodney King verdict, I went to school as usual. I could hear helicopters ominously flying overhead, but otherwise the campus was eerily calm. Around lunchtime, however, classes were abruptly canceled and we were told to go home. By then, we could see and smell the smoke wafting from Koreatown. My mother arrived to pick me up, looking tense and preoccupied. On the drive home, we took Third Street west, past the Original Farmers Market. Traffic was at a standstill. Crowds of people surged around the car, some pushing overflowing shopping carts, others hauling armfuls of clothing, boxes of diapers, electronics. On every block, we passed another building on fire—a Ross Dress for Less, a swap meet, a gas station. At home, we locked the doors and waited for my father, who arrived a few hours later. The unrest was spreading, and he had decided to close the store early. It was unnerving to see him at such an unusual hour—he usually returned home past midnight. While my sister and I watched the lurid footage on TV, my parents switched on Radio Korea and listened to live-broadcast messages from callers: *Please help us. Please pray for us.*

That night, my father stayed home. Over the next couple of days, I pleaded with him not to leave the house. Like all Korean men, he'd completed mandatory military service in the ROK Army and knew how to use a gun. Once, I'd found an unloaded pistol and a box of ammo hidden in his desk drawer, and I knew he sometimes kept a gun under the counter at work. I'd seen the footage of Korean men with their rifles on the roof of Hannam supermarket, and

I'd also seen photos of Eddie Song Lee's body crumpled in the street. I was fifteen years old. I didn't want my father to follow in Eddie's footsteps. I didn't want him to die.

I didn't know that, on the second or third night of the uprising, my parents got a phone call from the police. Someone had lit a garbage can on fire outside of their store, and the heat from the inferno had blown out the windows, setting off the alarms. The place was trashed, black soot everywhere, sludgy water, broken glass. My parents spent hours cleaning up the mess, putting up plywood as my sister and I slept. The Taco Bell and El Pollo Loco next door were still standing, but the Safeway and Thrifty across the parking lot had been looted. My parents didn't tell us about the damage. They came home, exhausted and filthy, but they kept it a secret. Thirty years later, when my mother finally told me this story as I was interviewing her for this book, she said, "We didn't tell you because we didn't want to give you fear."*

The LA Uprising was the primal scene of racial awakening—for myself and for the Korean American community. We were not white. We were not Black. We were caught somewhere in the middle, swept up in a twisted racial drama that was playing out on television screens across the country. From being invisible, we were now hypervisible, and not in a good way. We were portrayed as gun-toting vigilantes. Or we were cast as racist foreigners. Or we were depicted as wailing victims. For my parents, the 1992 LA Uprising (or sa-i-gu, as it was called in the Korean

---

* The Pioneer Chicken is now a Popeyes; the Safeway is now a Northgate Market; the Taco Bell is now a Yoshinoya Beef Bowl; the Thrifty is now a CVS. I have never been back. I know this from Google Earth.

community) destroyed the fantasy of America as a haven for immigrant strivers. We had been scapegoated once again, sacrificed for the country's unresolved racial sins.

My parents were among the lucky ones. My father did not die. My parents' store did not burn down. We did not go bankrupt. Yet the trauma lingered and festered. A survey taken in the aftermath of the unrest reported that 68 percent of Korean Americans thought things were going "badly" or "pretty badly" in their community, and 40 percent were considering leaving Los Angeles. In the aftermath of the uprising, many developed symptoms of hwa-byung—insomnia, depression, bewildered rage. Families fell apart, others found themselves homeless and destitute, still others battled addiction and despair.

In school, I'd been indoctrinated into the American dream, that "vast, moth-eaten musical brocade" pretending all men are created equal.* But I knew it was bullshit. Trapped at home, staring at the TV screen, I felt an overwhelming nausea, a mix of shame, complicity, and despair. My mother was around the same age as Soon Ja Du. My parents had once owned a liquor store, and I could imagine my own mother pulling a gun to shoot someone. I'd seen firsthand how the grinding hours, the lack of money, and the constant state of fear could turn my mother into something monstrous. My mother knew it, too. When Du received no jail time, my mother thanked God and Judge Karlin for their mercy.

On the other hand, I'd been born in this country, and though my face was Korean, I felt undeniably American. The outside world might see me as a model minority or

---

* Apologies to Philip Larkin.

an unassimilable alien, yet I saw myself as neither of these things. When I looked at Latasha Harlins, I saw someone my own age who had been wrongfully accused and tragically murdered. When I looked at Soon Ja Du, I saw someone abject and repulsive, someone I was desperate to distance myself from. Yet where did *I* fit in? Whose "side" was I on? The racial imaginary did not allow space for someone like me. I was a traitor and a turncoat, someone who could not be trusted by anyone—white, Black, or Korean.

A few years before the uprising, when I was thirteen years old, I got into an explosive fight with my mother, and she threw me out of the car near a police station (she was always threatening to turn me in to the police). It was dusk, and the sidewalk was empty except for commuters waiting for the bus and the occasional vagrant. I wandered into a nearby liquor store because I sure as hell wasn't going into the police station, and I had nowhere else to go. I had no cash on me, not even thirty-five cents for a candy bar, so I loitered in the aisles until the store owner accosted me and accused me of shoplifting. As I stood there stammering my innocence, he lifted my sweatshirt to pat me down. I can still feel his hands under my shirt, touching my bare skin. I fled the store in a vortex of shame, feeling violated and repulsed. But when I later told my mother what had happened, she was grimly unsympathetic. "Good," she said. "You deserved it. This is what happens when you act like a criminal."

What is the point of this story? I don't want to trivialize or personalize an unspeakable tragedy. I am not Latasha Harlins. My mother is not Soon Ja Du. I did not die because a storeowner mistakenly assumed I was shoplifting. I was protected by my face—my Korean face—and though I was groped, I was not murdered. My Asian-ness had offered me partial protection; it had offered me some privilege, as if on a sliding scale. It had offered Soon Ja Du the sympathy of a white judge and zero prison time. Yet it had not protected my parents' business from being torched. It had not prevented Koreatown from being devastated. It had not protected us from racism in America. Who was I? The monster or the victim? What if I were both?

I've come to realize my tortured relationship with my mother is a kind of allegory for my experience of race in this country. I saw my mother the way the racial imaginary had taught me to see her: as irredeemably foreign, a model minority stereotype, a monster, and a murderer. In my mind, she *was* Soon Ja Du. To become fully American, I had to reject her. And yet, if my mother was irredeemably foreign, then so was I. If she was a model minority stereotype, then so was I. If she was a monster and a murderer—then *so was I*. The racial imaginary saw us as one and the same. I could not escape the curse of race in America, just as I could not escape the curse of han. How would I reconcile my two warring selves without being torn apart?* I love my mother but I hate my mother. I love being Korean but I hate being Korean. I love America but I hate America.†

* * *

---

* As W. E. B. Du Bois writes, "One ever feels his two-ness, an American, a Negro, two souls, two thoughts, two unreconciled strivings, too many ideals in one dark body, whose dogged strength alone keeps it from being torn asunder."

† As Julia Kristeva writes, "We must abject the maternal, the object which has created us, in order to construct an identity."

I've long taught Toni Morrison's novel *Beloved*, one of the most powerful explorations of racial trauma I have ever read. Based on the true story of Margaret Garner, a fugitive slave who killed her own daughter rather than see her returned to slavery, *Beloved* depicts the reverberating effects of slavery and the slave trade on generations of Black Americans. Morrison employs the term "rememory" to describe how this trauma is a collective experience, a form of generational haunting. It haunts even those descendants who never personally experienced enslavement. It's comprised of no single memory but a compilation of memories—of violence, lynching, rape, dehumanization, and more. Rememories never die. They must be confronted in order to be exorcized.

Racial trauma is what Morrison calls an "unspeakable thing unspoken." A taboo. An inexpressible atrocity. In order to survive, you must will yourself to forget, to never speak of it again. But *not* speaking of the trauma is in some ways worse. Forgetting or repressing is only a temporary fix, a Band-Aid. The wound is still there. It festers. It gets worse. It's a no-win situation. Every act of speaking, every act of storytelling and testimony, is simultaneously an act of re-traumatization and an act of healing.

My family came to America to start over, to partake in an act of collective forgetting. They did not know about this country's history of Indigenous extermination, Black enslavement, and Asian exclusion. They had their own history to escape—the legacy of war and colonization. But rememories don't die. The LA Uprising was the collision of two historical traumas—of Black Americans in anguish over centuries of brutalization and murder of Black bodies, and of Korean Americans in anguish over centuries of subjugation and powerlessness. The more I think about it, the more I see rememory and han as conjoined. Both represent the collective inheritance of trauma and cultural genocide, passed down from generation to generation. Both can create glorious works of art, music, culture. Both can also kill you.

If the LA Uprising felt familiar, that's because it had happened before—during the 1967 riots in Newark, after the police beat John Smith, a Black cabdriver; during the 1965 Watts Riots, after the police beat Marquette Frye, a Black motorist; during the Chicago Race Riot of 1919, after police refused to arrest the white man who stoned Eugene Williams, a Black teenager, causing him to drown in Lake Michigan. The beating of Rodney King, the shooting of Latasha Harlins, these were not historic anomalies. They conjured the ghosts of past victims of racial violence, dehumanization, lynching, and social control stretching all the way back to slavery. Generations upon generations of unspeakable things unspoken.

In 1992, I saw the ghosts of my parents' past. I witnessed rememories of the Korean War in the images of men taking up arms, in Eddie Song Lee's crumpled body and his mother's grief, in the smoldering buildings and tanks rolling through the streets. I witnessed it in the upswell of bitterness within my community, the sense that we'd been fucked over again by the powerful. No one cared about saving Koreatown. No one cared about Koreans. My parents' generation had been lured to this country by Americans who'd "saved" them from communism, who'd promised a way out of poverty and oppression and their own historical trauma. They'd been duped.

The LA Uprising was a conflagration of han, an epic shit

show of han, when the curse of being Korean collided with the curse of being American. Elaine Kim calls it the Korean community's "baptism" and "initiation" into becoming American, but it was more akin to waterboarding. Welcome to America, our great dysfunctional family. Welcome to our sordid secrets and our unatoned-for sins. This wasn't a baptism. This was torture.

* * *

The LA Uprising officially lasted six days. One week after the verdict, I returned to school. Although the unrest had come within blocks of my high school, the neighborhood around campus was pristine and untouched, the mansions still standing, the lawns still green. The mayor, Tom Bradley, lived in one of those homes, a massive Tudor on the edge of Koreatown, in spitting distance of some of the worst destruction. The cops had formed a line of defense along Crenshaw Boulevard to prevent any of the destruction from creeping west. That's where they'd been instead of protecting businesses a few blocks away.

I felt like I was having an out-of-body experience. On campus, people talked about the uprising like it was an abstract thing. My white classmates lived in places like Beverly Hills and Bel-Air, where they'd been shielded from the violence, yet they acted as if hordes of Black and brown people were about to knock down their front doors. I heard rumors that a school parent had hosted the Brentwood fundraiser where LAPD Chief Daryl Gates was caught eating canapés while the city was going up in flames. I remember only *one* adult at school asking if my family and I were OK. She was the head of the upper school and came from a

WASPy family who summered on Nantucket. Seeing me in the hallway, she asked, "How is your family? Is their store safe?" I was surprised she even knew my parents owned a business. "They're fine," I told her, and she didn't pry. Deep down, I was grateful to her for asking, but mostly I felt exposed. People were talking about us. We were the objects of pity and judgment.

In the months following the LA Uprising, business at my parents' store continued to slide. Their main source of revenue was from the lunch rush, as crowds of students from the local high school, Leuzinger, poured into the store during their lunch hour. But Leuzinger High was a microcosm of the racial and ethnic tensions facing the entire Los Angeles region. White flight and an influx of Asian and Latinx immigrants had transformed the community from a predominantly white neighborhood—a historic sundown town and the birthplace of the Beach Boys—to one that was primarily Black and brown.* Left behind to fight over dwindling resources, students splintered into warring groups. In 1990, a Filipino student was killed in a drive-by shooting by a Vietnamese gang member as payback for a beating that had occurred on school grounds. The following year, a fight broke out on campus, turning into a full-fledged brawl involving dozens of students and hundreds of spectators.

My parents' store was a block away from Leuzinger High, and my parents occasionally employed Leuzinger students as cashiers. In the months leading up to the Uprising, a fight between gang members broke out in the park-

---

* Like Inglewood a few miles north, Hawthorne was originally a sundown town—meaning that if you were Black, you were not welcome to live there or even to be around after dark.

ing lot outside my parents' store. A crowd gathered and someone was thrown through the store window, shattering it. The police and paramedics were called, and my parents spent the rest of the day cleaning up blood and glass. Fights were happening constantly now, so in the year following the LA Uprising, school administrators locked down the campus. They installed metal detectors, hired more armed officers, and erected a fence around campus greased with axle oil to prevent trespassers from getting in—or students from getting out.

Leuzinger became a virtual prison. As part of the lockdown, school administrators banned students from leaving campus at lunchtime, which meant business owners like my parents saw their sales evaporate. The district invited the bigger and more popular fast-food vendors such as McDonald's and Taco Bell to set up shop on campus, allowing them to make up for some of their lost business. Pioneer Chicken wasn't one of them. It was already a reject fast-food option—if you were a student, you went there when the lines were too long at Taco Bell or you didn't have enough money for a Big Mac—so there was no respite for my parents. They were fucked.

My parents had sent me to a fancy private school precisely because they did not want me to attend a school like Leuzinger. They wanted me to have the privileges and protections of whiteness. But by the time I was a senior, I was desperate to get out. The white girls at my school were doing beautification projects, painting murals on the side of the 10 freeway with birds and butterflies to symbolize LA rising from the ashes. Every time I passed that mural, I wanted to stab myself in the face. The past was being whitewashed right before my eyes. I lived in a city that supposedly had no history, where nobodies from nowhere could remake themselves into tycoons and movie stars. The LA Uprising was just another part of the inconvenient past that could be spackled over and forgotten.

When I reflect on the collective experience of trauma after the riots, I don't think of the burned-out buildings and the individual, spectacular moments of suffering—I think of the everyday, invisible acts of post-traumatic survival. My mother trying to cut costs by limiting customers to *one* napkin and *one* ketchup packet each. (This did not go over well.) My father getting a ticket for reckless driving, not because he was drunk (as the officer suspected) but because he was bone tired, and that's why his car kept drifting out of its lane. My mother taking me to the Salvation Army to shop for clothes, where we bumped into two of my classmates who were thrifting (this was the grunge era, when it was "cool" for rich girls to look poor, but it was not cool to actually *be* poor).

I applied to a bunch of prestigious schools back east, all with outlandish tuition my parents could not afford. I remember filling out the torturously bureaucratic FAFSA form and getting to the final section, where there was a box for additional comments. My father laboriously drafted a few sentences on the back of an envelope and handed it to me to fix the grammar. I ended up writing something along the lines of, "My parents are self-employed small business owners. Their business has been severely affected by the recession. We ask that you consider their situation when determining our financial need." I tried to make it sound as clinical as possible because I didn't want to sound like we were begging. (We were begging.)

Of all the schools I got into, Princeton was the farthest away, the most prestigious, and offered the most amount of financial aid. When I graduated, I was voted Most Likely to Go Away, Stay Away, Far Away.

Part II

SHAME

Chapter Six

IN LOCO PARENTIS

In 2000, Elizabeth Shin, a nineteen-year-old Korean American student at MIT, died after setting herself on fire in her dorm room. She was the daughter of Cho and Kisuk Shin, Korean immigrants who settled in West Orange, New Jersey, where they raised their three children. Elizabeth was their oldest, an academic superstar who graduated salutatorian of her high school class. She was also a perfectionist who panicked when she failed physics her first semester of college and overdosed on pills (she said it was an accident). To her therapists, she admitted cutting herself and struggling with anxiety and depression. To her parents, she insisted that she was fine and that they shouldn't worry.

After Shin's apparent suicide, her parents sued the school, claiming the university had an obligation to serve in loco parentis and had failed to inform them of their daughter's mental health struggles. MIT countered that Shin had a history of mental illness and self-harm going back to high school, and that they should not be held responsible for her death. In 2006, the Shins and MIT settled the case for an undisclosed amount, mutually agreeing the incident was likely a "tragic accident," not a suicide.

Who was to blame for Shin's death? Although the settlement absolved MIT of legal responsibility, it didn't stop the avalanche of blame that followed the tragedy. University lawyers argued that Shin was mentally ill and had already attempted suicide several times in the past. Despite the efforts of administrators and psychiatrists, she was determined to kill herself and eventually succeeded. Others blamed Shin's parents for being hard-ass Korean immigrants who demanded excellence from their daughter and aggravated her feelings of worthlessness and inadequacy. A friend of Shin's claimed she "hated" her parents. Still others focused on MIT's reputation for being a pressure cooker full of maladjusted overachievers. The *Boston Globe* reported that MIT had a "culture of suicide," with a suicide rate almost three times the national average for college undergraduates. Upper-middle-class parents had entered an arms race of test prep, enrichment classes, tutors, extracurriculars, and internships to get their children into increasingly selective and pricey elite colleges. Their kids were referred to as "teacups," liable to "crack" at any minute.

The reporter Deborah Sontag goes through all of these possibilities in her 2002 *New York Times* article "Who Was Responsible for Elizabeth Shin?" Most of the hypotheses revolve around accusations of bad parenting. Shin's parents were crappy parents because they were immigrant strivers who pushed her too hard and alienated her. MIT was a crappy surrogate parent because it fostered a toxic culture and offered insufficient mental health resources. This entire generation of American parents were crappy parents because they acted like helicopters/lawn mowers and raised depressed, unhappy kids.

Buried in Sontag's article was another possibility, briefly voiced by Shin's father and then anxiously downplayed by her mother. As a senior at West Orange High School, Shin should have been valedictorian based on her GPA but was disqualified for missing a physics test and never making it up. During his interview with Sontag, Shin's father admitted wondering whether racism had been the reason behind his daughter's being bumped from the valedictorian spot. He contemplated suing the high school but worried about jeopardizing his son's chances when he graduated the following year. (His son ended up co-valedictorian with "let's say, two white girls," Shin's father said.)

Sontag describes how Shin's mother looked "fretful" as her husband spoke, worrying that he shouldn't have been so frank. She writes, "[Mrs. Shin] didn't want him to come across as overly concerned with his children's success or paranoid or litigious."

Mrs. Shin's worries about how they were perceived struck me as painfully familiar. She knew they'd be caricatured by the defense, and she knew what stereotypes they'd deploy. Mr. Shin would be depicted as the psycho Korean dad, the model minority gone amok. Or he would be depicted as a "paranoid" person of color, seeing racism where it didn't exist. Or he'd be depicted as a rapacious opportunist, looking for a quick payday.

She also knew they'd be caricatured by the white American public, reading this article written by a white reporter in the pages of the white *New York Times*. I cringed as Sontag transcribed Mr. Shin's awkward English and noted Mrs.

Shin's "disconcerting" habit of speaking of her daughter in the present tense, which she then acknowledged was probably "largely a language issue." No shit.

Elizabeth Shin was a few years younger than me. She died two years after I graduated from college, and I recognized in her my own struggles with anxiety and depression, the way I used achievement to paper over feelings of inadequacy and my own complicated relationship with my parents. I could relate to the pressures of attending an elite school and feeling like I was the only one who was struggling. I'd never been suicidal in the way Shin was suicidal—I'd never OD'd on drugs, I'd never cut my wrists, and I'd never accidentally-on-purpose set myself on fire. But, to borrow Kiese Laymon's phrase, I was very well practiced in the art of slowly killing myself in America.

* * *

When I was applying to college, I initially wanted to go to schools like UCLA and UC Berkeley—prestigious public universities with large Asian American student bodies.* You would have thought my mother would be supportive, but oh no. One of her concerns was that these schools were "too Asian," and that I would get lost in the masses of Asian-ness. She wanted me to attend a predominantly white institution where I could more successfully be recognized for myself, not my race.† Of course, I yelled at my mom that she was a self-hating Asian. Didn't she care about me finding friends with shared racial experiences and awareness? Wasn't she

---

* I did not end up applying to UCLA because I would have rather died than stay so close to home.

† She also thought Berkeley was a hotbed of Communists and hippies.

perpetuating the racist beliefs that "all Asians look alike" and implying there was such a thing as "too many Asians"?

At the time, UCLA was known (and is probably still known) as "University of Caucasians Lost Among Asians." The most recent demographic data states that 39 percent of the student body is Asian American/Pacific Islander, 31 percent is white, 20 percent is Latinx, 4 percent is Black, and less than 1 percent is Indigenous. This is in a city that, according to the 2020 Census, is 26 percent non–Hispanic/Latinx white, 8 percent Black, 15 percent Asian, and 48 percent Latinx. Asian Americans are not only overrepresented at UCLA, but they are also the single largest demographic.

My family had lived through the anti-Asian sentiment that accompanied Japan's rise in economic power in the 1980s, and we were now living through the anti-Asian sentiment that resulted from growing numbers of Asian immigrants "invading" previously all-white spaces. Yes, my mother was parroting white supremacist beliefs, but she was also trying to protect me and warn me. She saw how we were treated by a white majority culture that saw us as a threat. There were too many of "us," and we threatened to displace white people as the majority. What would happen next? Would we wrest power from white people? Turn the campus into a mini-Asia? Replace white supremacy with Asian supremacy?

Safety might come in numbers, but when it came to minoritized people in white spaces, so did the fierceness of the white backlash. For my mother, it was better for me to be one Asian in a sea of whiteness (the token) than to be one in a sea of Asians. In the former case, I'd be seen as less of a threat to whiteness and presumably receive more favorable treatment by the dominant culture. In the latter, I'd be anonymized and dehumanized. Who's to blame for this kind of minoritized thinking—the minoritized person, or the culture in which they must learn to survive? The messenger (my mother) or the sender (white supremacy)?

Ironically, my mother's great hope—that I would be less dehumanized in an environment where I was perceived as less of a threat—did not come to pass. If anything, I felt even more anonymous, more unseen at Princeton, where the percentage of Asian American students was unofficially pegged around 20 percent.* Coming from the West Coast, where Asian people and Asian culture at least had a longer history and presence, I now entered a space that was so overwhelmingly white—in culture *and* in fact—that I felt like I was drowning. I was an Asian lost among Caucasians.

* * *

I went to college to get away from my parents, so I was puzzled and amused when I saw kids whose parents were around *all the time*, helping them move into their dorm and then dropping by during the school year for football games or parents' weekend or just to take them out for a fancy meal. I knew kids who went home every weekend to do their laundry or to escape their roommates for forty-eight hours. My roommate was from a town forty-five minutes away from campus. We were both Asian American, played

---

* In her book *Just Us: An American Conversation* (2020), the poet Claudia Rankine sits next to a white man on a flight who complains that "the Asians are flooding the Ivy Leagues." Apparently, even 20 percent is intolerable to white supremacy.

a musical instrument, and were on financial aid, so when the housing office gave out roommate assignments, they probably thought we'd be a good fit.

We were not a good fit. I arrived on campus alone; she arrived with her parents and sister and what seemed like a whole slew of friends she already knew from high school and the pre-Juilliard program in New York City. In the first ten minutes of meeting her, I discovered that (1) she was pissed she was at Princeton because she'd *really* wanted to go to Harvard, where her older sister was a junior, but she'd been wait-listed, (2) she was horrified at how small our cinder block dorm room was, and how we had to share a communal bathroom with ten other girls, and (3) she was horrified at sharing this tiny dorm room with *me* because she'd grown up in a big suburban house with her own bedroom that was double the size of this shoebox.

My roommate's parents did everything for her, including buying her a top-of-the-line Power Mac and setting it up for her (I didn't have a computer yet, so she briefly let me check my email—then a novelty—on her machine, until I apparently "broke" it and was forbidden from touching it again). She took one look at the bunk bed setup and asked for the bottom bunk, which I said was fine because I grew up sharing a room with my sister, and we had always slept on bunk beds. (I actually thought this college bunk bed setup was an improvement on my home situation because the bunk bed my sister and I shared for fifteen years had a big WARNING tag on the frame that said the top bunk was only safe for children up to sixty-five pounds, and my sister and I were basically double that weight. It's a miracle it didn't pancake us.)

I was a terrible roommate, too. I broke her computer,* I was disgustingly messy,† and I once placed a hot iron face-down on the carpet, leaving a perfect torpedo-shaped burn mark behind. Our hallmates got used to hearing us bitch about each other. There were maybe twenty-five people total on our hall, and I became friends with half of them. Our immediate next-door neighbors were two white guys who were eighteen but looked middle-aged. One was already sporting extreme male-pattern baldness; the other wore Nantucket red pants and belts with embroidered whales. They played lacrosse and blasted Pearl Jam 24/7. Their room smelled like ass.‡ Down the hall, there were two "psycho singles," one occupied by a trustfundian, the other by a surly hipster. Most people were stuck with one roommate or several their first year of college, but some "special" cases got their own rooms. I rarely saw either of them because they were always in New York clubbing or too strung out to leave their rooms.

My hall was probably 20 percent Asian American, and we ran the gamut from AJ, a South Asian guy from Connecticut who had anglicized his name and dated only white blond girls, to Priscilla, the Korean American daughter of a doctor from upstate New York, who affected a British accent and spent hours in the bathroom doing her makeup and curling her hair, to Angie, a Hong Kong immigrant who wore zero makeup and was singularly focused on landing a

---

* I still maintain I was unfairly maligned for the computer incident.

† She was messy, too, but she would pile all her shit on her bed whereas I couldn't do that because remember? I got stuck with the top bunk. We were cited by the fire inspectors multiple times because our room was so slovenly it was considered a fire hazard.

‡ If you've seen the movie *Get Out*, they looked like the inbred lacrosse bro.

job in investment banking (she's now the head of the Asia Pacific division of a major New York bank). I learned for the first time that there were differences between East Coast and West Coast Asian Americans, and midwestern and southern Asian Americans, and that the farther east or south you went, the more diffuse Asian American identity seemed to get. Those of us who were born and raised in Hawaii and California, where we were a majority or a substantial minority, were like fire-breathing radicals compared to those who were raised in, say, Oklahoma or Rhode Island as the only Asian family in town. The racism I encountered in Princeton was also different. It was much more overt, ham-handed, crude.

I'd never left Los Angeles before, and I naively assumed a place like Princeton, situated an hour away from New York City and an hour away from Philadelphia, would more or less approximate my experience, if not in LA, then at least at my high school. But Princeton seemed even more backward, more black-and-white (literally), a throwback to a previous century. I didn't know it then, but Princeton had a reputation as the "southernmost" of the Ivies, with a legacy of educating members of the wealthy, white plantocracy.* It *felt* southern in its conservative gentility, its bucolic landscape, even its veneration of Woodrow Wilson, a southerner and former college president who championed segregation and white supremacy. Coupled with the school's straight-up WASP/prep school heritage (which it shared with the other Ivy League schools), the university was steeped in a culture of white supremacy.

Nowhere was that more evident than in the eating club

---

* University of Pennsylvania is geographically the farthest south of all Ivy League institutions, but culturally, Princeton is considered the most "southern."

scene, the center of social *and* dining life at the school.*
Around *70 percent* of juniors and seniors belonged to an
eating club, and half of them were selective and operated
more like private societies than cafeterias. From their incep-
tion in the late nineteenth century, the eating clubs were
built on segregation and social stratification. You ate and
socialized with people who were "like" you, and funnily
enough, it perpetuated the racial dynamics of Jim Crow.
At the snootiest eating clubs on Prospect Avenue, housed
in plantation-style mansions built in the Greek revival and
Georgian styles, the dining rooms were like a throwback
to the antebellum era, with a (mostly) white and privileged
student body served formal, sit-down meals by a (mostly)
Black staff in uniforms.

As one student noted in a 2019 *New York Times* article,
"The eating club system de facto segregates. And this country has a long dark history of using dining as a social sorting
system." Even Woodrow Wilson, that old racist, loathed
the eating club system, calling it "snobbish" and deeming
the social plight of the rejected (white, often Jewish) 30
percent "little less than deplorable." Eighty years later, if
you were part of the deplorables who didn't join an eating
club—many of whom were first-gen, BIPOC, low-income
students—you could either go "independent" (living in a
suite with a kitchen so you could cook for yourself), join a
co-op, or forage for food on your own. You could continue
to eat at the dining hall if you wanted, but good luck seeing

---

* In their first two years, undergraduates lived in "colleges," or dormitories with
attached dining halls. In their last two years, students moved into upperclass-
men housing and the majority joined eating clubs, which charged dining and
social dues.

any of your friends. You were outside the social caste system; you were literally an out-caste.*

Princeton was promoted as an immense banquet for those of us who were lucky enough to be admitted. There was seemingly so much wealth and abundance and choice. There was money to do research abroad, there were Nobel Prize–winning professors, there was the promise of status and pedigree and social mobility. But the whole system was built upon whiteness and in service of whiteness. The school was founded to educate the white elite, and it remains that way, even when the definition of "elite" has expanded slightly to include nonwhite people. To be successful at Princeton was to be indoctrinated into this culture. BIPOC folks who graduate from Princeton go on to be highly successful in the rarefied, white worlds of law, government, finance, medicine, academia. It's like a finishing school, where you learn how to sit at the table of power and how to use the right fork.

Who is let in? Who is kept out? The door was open much wider for certain groups—"legacies," as the children of predominantly white and privileged alums were called, as well as for athletes, who also skewed white (because who else plays squash?). If your dad—and it was always your dad when I was there, since Princeton didn't go coed until 1969—went to Princeton, your chances of getting in to the school were four times higher than that of a nonlegacy. Meanwhile, recruited athletes made up roughly 20 percent of the entering class at Ivy League universities and the top liberal arts colleges. Added to the 15 percent of the entering class who were legacies (and assuming little/no overlap

---

* See also Jennifer Miller, "Takeover at Princeton's Quadrangle," *New York Times*, Dec. 12, 2019.

between the two populations), nearly half of the slots in each incoming class were already filled before the "general" student pool was considered.

I used to think my getting into Princeton was a meritocratic triumph—that I had worked my ass off and had "deserved" to get in based on my grades, my test scores, my clear awesomeness, and my model minority-ness. But now I realize that it was more accurately a reflection of my relative privilege. Sure, I wasn't a legacy, I wasn't an athlete, I wasn't white, and I wasn't in the one percent. But I had the luxury of piano and ballet lessons, private schools, white adjacency, and immigrant parents whose single-minded desire was to get me into a school like Princeton. When I arrived, I was shocked to realize that while there were a lot of brilliant people, there were also a lot of really mediocre people at Princeton. As Michelle Obama, a Princeton alum, once observed, "I have been at every powerful table you can think of . . . [and] they are not that smart."

Some of them knew it, too. I remember a white hockey recruit drunkenly bragging that he was "the dumbest student at Princeton," because not only was he an athlete and thus subject to less stringent admissions requirements, but he was also *Canadian*, so the standardized testing bar was set even lower for him. I don't remember any legacies openly conceding their advantages, probably because they felt entitled to attend the same school as their dads and grandfathers. In any case, my sense that Princeton students were socioeconomically privileged is borne out by the statistics. According to a 2017 study in the *New York Times*, the median family income of a student at Princeton is $186,100, and 72 percent come from the top 20 percent. Only 2.2 percent of students come from the bottom 20 percent.

Getting into Princeton was only one gate. Once you got in, there were many more, each granting you access to ever more rarefied circles, each whiter than the one before. Maybe it was getting into a selective major. Or getting into a selective eating club or fraternity/sorority. Or landing a coveted summer internship at a bank. Or on and on and on. There is always another gate, and each admits fewer and fewer people, until soon you have the ruling class of this country, where the "faces of power," as the *New York Times* calls it, are 80 percent white. If my high school taught me how to be successful in a predominantly white Ivy League school, Princeton taught me how to be successful in a predominantly white world beyond college. And at each stage, the competition for the trappings of whiteness, for token status, for acceptance into the elite and its network of social connections, became fiercer among the BIPOC students who had made it that far.

In the years since I've graduated, the school has made some efforts to make dining more "inclusive"—by keeping the cafeterias open over holiday breaks; by opening up a four-year dining hall; by giving more financial aid to students who wish to join an eating club with its higher dining fees and social dues. Some of the clubs aren't selective, though they are still self-sorting, and you have to feel comfortable hanging out with its members and paying its fees. I've read of first-gen, low-income (FLI) students "taking over" one of the eating clubs to make it more welcoming to students previously ignored by the system. But all of it seems like a Band-Aid to the incorrigible fact that Princeton's dining and social culture is built on segregation, and that segregation is racialized.

The one place I found a community at Princeton was in the dining hall. That's where many BIPOC students who weren't rich worked and ate. Lots of students tried their mightiest to get out of their PUDS* assignment, seeing it as menial labor. My roommate was one of them, finagling a job at the music library, where she mostly checked out opera scores to grad students. But the dining hall jobs paid more, and the dish room—the hardest, dirtiest work—paid the most. The first week of school, I showed up for my scheduled 6:00 A.M. shift, dressed as instructed in a ratty T-shirt, jeans, and sneakers. My parents were in food service, so I figured I already had some skills under my belt. I knew how to prep orders and I knew my way around a walk-in refrigerator. How bad could it be?

* * *

It turns out that working the dish room is fucking hard work. There's a reason why my dad and probably a zillion other immigrants with iffy English and few marketable skills end up starting there. You're standing on your feet for hours, scraping food off plates and stacking trays and glasses and dishes into the industrial dishwasher, hauling heavy flats of clean glasses off the conveyor belt. During the lunch and din-

---

* Princeton University Dining Services, or PUDS, is a great example of onomatopoeia. It sounds like "dud," or "plod," or "putz." If you said you worked at PUDS, it sounded like you were basically saying you were a loser. It's now been renamed the more mellifluous PCD (Princeton Campus Dining).

ner rush, you're scrambling to prevent a pileup, kind of like
Lucy and Ethel at the candy factory—except instead of chocolate bonbons, you're dealing with chunks of Happy Family
and congealed chicken cordon bleu. It was a million degrees
in the dish room, and you always smelled like steamed garbage at the end of your shift.

My parents worked like dogs at their store and were
always coming home with hot oil burns on their arms and
reeking of fried chicken, yet here I was at a swanky Ivy
League university, doing three-hour shifts in the dining
hall and getting my ass kicked. No wonder my parents
didn't want me to follow in their footsteps. In high school,
I'd occasionally helped my parents at the store, but they
always had me do the easy stuff like filling sodas, assem-
bling meals, and calling out order numbers.* I was a total
marshmallow.

At one of my first shifts, I met Renée, a junior premed student who worked the breakfast shifts at my dorm. In the first
five minutes of chatting, we discovered that we were both
from LA and that Renée had graduated from Leuzinger. I
was so sheltered and naive and, yes, racist that I just assumed
someone like Renée wouldn't end up at a place like Princeton. I told her my parents' store was around the corner from
her high school and inwardly shrank a little, wondering if
she assumed they were "the racist Koreans" caricatured by
the media. But Renée didn't seem to know of their store or
maybe she did but didn't care, and I breathed a sigh of relief.

---

* I'm sure my parents were breaking child labor laws because I was definitely
younger than sixteen. My friend Eileen routinely worked the register at her
parents' liquor store when she was underage, but she was tall and could pass
for older. I, on the other hand, looked like a baby.

She was the first person who made me feel welcome and did not judge me the way I had been taught to judge myself and others. We often worked the morning shifts together, and she showed me how to refill the cereal and milk dispensers. When I asked her why she didn't work the dish room, she told me it would mess up her hair.

The dining hall wasn't perfect, but at least for the first two years of college, everyone had to eat there. People complained about the food all the time, but I was bowled over by the sheer abundance and variety. After years of eating leftover Pioneer Chicken, I couldn't believe how many choices I had—I could order a burger at the grill, or sample four different hot entreés, or make myself a salad, or just eat cereal and frozen yogurt. If I wanted to, I could go back for seconds and thirds. In the older, neo-Gothic dining halls, I could sit under stained glass windows and chandeliers, eating at long wood tables and imagining I was at Oxford or Cambridge.

Even then, it was a thinly veiled facade. Work-study students and full-time food service employees washed dishes and served food, hovering at the margins, marked by racial and class difference. In the classroom, we were supposedly equals, supposedly allowed access to the privilege of a Princeton education. Outside, that fantasy of democracy evaporated, as we were segregated into those who served and those who were served. My friend Alejandra, who worked the dish room at a different dining hall, watched as a group of white frat bros dumped bottles of ketchup and syrup into bowls and then sent them down the conveyor belt, laughing as she tried to clear the tray and the contents splattered all over her. My friend Naoko, who worked in the same dining hall as Alejandra, was transferred to the Center for Jewish Life's kosher dining hall and felt secretly relieved that she would no longer have to serve the students living in her dorm.

I don't want it to sound like working in the dining hall was endless, humiliating drudgery. Kitchen culture is raucous and profane and hilarious, and it welcomes misfits and oddballs. Before kale became an aspirational, wellness-industry superfood, we used its frilly pink-and-green leaves to "decorate" the salad bar and hot food line, where it would wilt and look increasingly unappetizing. We would add cherry tomato eyes and carrot-top noses and radishes carved into roses, and soon little compost sculptures would appear with messages we printed out with the label maker: TRY THE SLOPPY JOE! IT TASTES BETTER THAN IT LOOKS! At brunch, we had push-up contests in between serving slices of ham and roast beef, and the omelet bar guy set up a boom box and practiced his stand-up routine on captive customers/classmates. The kitchen staff would cook its own, tastier family meal before the dining hall doors opened—Haitian food, soul food—food that was totally different from the bland country club/hotel/institutional food we were serving.

The dining crew was a subculture at Princeton, and those of us who worked there created a different kind of social network. There was Reggie, a stocky, red-haired student manager who was Puerto Rican and from the Bronx and who would call and wake me up whenever I overslept my alarm (which happened more than I'd like to admit. I was an unreliable employee, the bane of my parents' existence). He was an economics major and helped me pass Econ 101 by tutoring me during my shift ("What's the demand curve?" he'd quiz me. "What is marginal utility?"), and he ended up getting a job on Wall Street, where I truly hope he went on to make a billion dollars.

Then there was Mrs. Williams, a full-time employee who had worked at our dining hall for years. In LA, the people who worked in kitchens and back of the house were mostly Latinx. At Princeton, the full-time food service workers were mostly Black. At my dining hall, many employees lived in Trenton, a majority-Black city ten miles away from Princeton. That's where Mrs. Williams lived, commuting to campus every morning before dawn with her husband, who worked as a cook at a different dorm. A freckled Black woman in her sixties with reading glasses hanging from her neck, Mrs. Williams was the senior-most member of the dining staff and in charge of swiping people's cards at the entrance to the servery. The other students complained about Mrs. Williams all the time because she never waved them in if they forgot their ID card, no matter how much they wheedled or yelled— she just looked at them, dead-eyed, and soon students learned not to even try. During lulls in service, Renée and I would chat with Mrs. Williams about our families or her retirement plans (Florida or bust) or the latest exam we were studying for. Mrs. Williams would worry we weren't dressed warmly enough for the winter (we were hopeless California girls) or try to convince us to try seitan (she was a Seventh-day Adventist and a strict vegetarian).

Mrs. Williams and the rest of the dining crew created an alternate family for me at Princeton, a group of people who looked out for me in the absence of my actual family. Both Reggie and Renée hooked me up with a coveted Reunions job, where students could make extra money by working as servers during the big, splashy dinners held by alumni classes. The fiftieth reunion was held in the courtyard outside my dormitory, and every year, after the end of classes, a large tent would go up, along with a dance floor and a dais for a live band that played Glenn Miller standards. We would serve limp salads and rubbery chicken to old white men wearing loud orange reunion jackets, along with their white-haired wives (or sometimes much younger second or third wives). Serve left, clear right, keep it moving. Renée got a hold of the label maker and gave us all fake names for our name tags. She was JEWEL. I was JASMINE. We would smile and lie when these doddering old men would ask us, "So, Jewel, what is your major?" or "Jasmine, what a pretty name! What year will you graduate?" Over the three-day Reunions weekend, we would work the dinner shift, then sneak into the Reunions parties, crashing the dance floors and scrounging for beer along the way.

Reggie and Renée had made a space for themselves outside the social caste system at Princeton, tapping the privileges of whiteness (a pipeline to Wall Street and med school; well-paying Reunions jobs; a fancy degree) while finding their community elsewhere. In retrospect, I should have followed their lead. But they were graduating, and I did not want to remain in the margins of campus social life.

By the beginning of my sophomore year, I had made my decision. I wanted to fit in and assimilate into the majority culture. So I decided to do what I had been trained to do. I tried to integrate myself into a social system that did not want me.

Chapter Seven

THE GLASS CEILING

Fool me once, shame on you
Fool me twice, shame on me
Fool my thrice, shame on me
Shame on me
Shame on me
Shame on me

Hazing is ritualized degradation, humiliation, and abuse. Usually you hear it in the context of sororities and fraternities, the military, gangs, boarding schools, or any social group based on hierarchy and exclusion and power. But hazing is everywhere, and white supremacy is a particularly vicious and unrelenting form of hazing. Microaggressions, racial epithets, hate crimes—all of these are just the ritualized abuses of white supremacy. It's putting you in your proper place, reminding you of who's really in power, and tempting you with the promise that one day you, too, might have the power to haze those weaker than you. And it's not just physical. It's social and psychological.

My first two years of college, I submitted to the hazing.

I wanted to join the club. I felt grateful even to be admitted. I studied the shibboleths of whiteness—how to dress, how to talk, how to project a sense of entitlement and superiority. Part of the code was never to acknowledge there was a code. Whiteness was invisible and normative. Privilege was invisible and normative. The term "privilege" didn't even exist in the context we use it today. No one ever said, "check your privilege," or used the term "white privilege." No one talked about whiteness at all. It was like fight club, but white club.

My sophomore year, I took a class in U.S. social history and was assigned Vance Packard's 1959 book, *The Status Seekers*, an exploration of class stratification in America. In one section, Packard analyzed the eating club system at Princeton in the 1950s, when clubs were a social sorting system for the white male elite. The clubs were no longer all-white, or all-male, but they retained much of the same reputation in the 1990s as they had in the 1950s. "Do you guys think this is still in effect today? The same social hierarchy and sorting?" our teaching assistant asked, lobbing us a softball question. Crickets. Maybe no one had done the reading, but Princeton students are adept at bullshitting and kissing ass, so the silence seemed purposeful. No one wanted to acknowledge the elephant in the room: despite efforts to "diversify" and "democratize," the social life at Princeton was still rooted in power, abuse, and hierarchy.

I was complicit as well. In my first two years at Princeton, I followed the script. I went to Prospect Avenue and tried to sneak my way into the clubs. I drank a lot of cheap beer in crowded taprooms and barfed in a lot of bathrooms. I joined a sorority that was mostly white, I joined a dance company that was mostly white, I tried to bicker (rush) an eating club that was mostly white and known to be the most "southern" of all the clubs. F. Scott Fitzgerald, my favorite writer when I was in high school, had been a member of this eating club and begun writing his first novel, *This Side of Paradise*, in its library. More than anything, I wanted to imagine myself in his company.

During the bicker process, I was paired with Karen, a mediocre white girl I'd gone to high school with who had been recruited to play tennis. Karen was blond, with a DD chest, which garnered her a popularity in college she had not enjoyed at our all-girls school. She ordered me to lick spilled beer off the bar, and I did it. She ordered me to lick whipped cream off the neck of another club member, a Black upper-classman who was on the basketball team and one of their token nonwhite members. In other words, a white woman ordered an Asian woman to lick whipped cream off a Black man, solely for her own amusement. Again, I did it. I never said no. I submitted to my own degradation.

I was rejected from the club, and that was the queasy, shame-filled moment when I realized all that hazing hadn't been intended to build solidarity and "initiate" me into a group. It had been intended to do the opposite, to shame me and to put me in my rightful place. It had just made explicit and visible what was implicit and invisible. If I'd been accepted, I know I would have kept up the charade—I would have thrilled at making it past another gate and entering an exclusive space, and then I would have become a gatekeeper myself and policed other people's access to that space. I remember some people who had been hosed (that is, rejected, but what an *interesting* choice of words) trying again and again to bicker a club only to be rejected over and over again. It felt so undignified, so desperate . . . and yet I was no different from them. I'd been programmed my whole life to finagle my way into spaces that did not want me.

I know college kids are insecure messes, desperate to fit in and belong—to remake themselves—and that kids who come from minoritized backgrounds feel this even more acutely. Still, I beat myself up for being seduced, for being duped. How dumb could I be? Why didn't I go where I was wanted? Why did I *willingly* put myself into this situation? I *hate* the person I once was. But then I remind myself: *You were brainwashed. You were young. You were trying to survive.*

The other day, I was talking to a friend of mine. She is a Black feminist and a professor on the East Coast. A Chinese American grad student in her class came to her office hours and admitted that when she was in high school, she and her friends all "wanted to be white." My friend stopped her. "No, you didn't," she said. "No one wants to be white. You wanted to be *human*." I had to steady myself. I'd always thought of my time at Princeton as a shameful pursuit of whiteness. But I did not want to be white. I wanted to be treated like white people got to be treated. I wanted to be treated like a human being.

* * *

In 2013, Chun "Michael" Deng, a nineteen-year-old student at Baruch College, died of traumatic brain injuries while being hazed by members of his Asian American fraternity, Pi Delta Psi. The only child of Chinese immigrants, Deng grew up within the "Asian bubble of Queens," as Jay Caspian Kang describes it, and attended Bronx High School of Science before matriculating at Baruch College, a commuter school in Manhattan and part of the CUNY system. In the first few months of his freshman year, Deng decided to pledge Pi Delta Psi, one of two Asian American fraternities on campus. According to Kang, Asian American fraternities and sororities emerged in the 1980s as a result of a growing political awareness and a sense of alienation among Asian Americans on college campuses. Fraternities like Pi Delta Psi taught their members about the history of anti-Asian discrimination in the United States and gave them a sense of shared identity and lineage. Participating in rituals of male bonding and brotherhood also provided a way of combating the emasculation Asian American men felt in American culture. After all, what's the opposite of the Asian nerd stereotype? An Asian bro.

Deng died while undergoing a hazing ritual called "the Glass Ceiling" and wearing a backpack in which he had stashed some notes on the history of Asian American oppression. He was tackled by his fraternity brothers— Asian American men—who body-slammed him over and over again, reenacting the brutal journey he would face in the white world as he tried to ascend the power hierarchy. They called him racial epithets—"chink" and "gook." They wanted him to imagine the racial abuses his immigrant parents faced, their sacrifices and humiliations on his behalf. His frat brothers were trying to toughen him up; they were trying to "help" him; they were trying to establish solidarity in suffering. But in the end, they killed him. In the end, *they* did the work of white supremacy.

Deng didn't try to join an all-white or majority-white

fraternity. He stayed close to home, dated a girl who was a member of an Asian American sorority, had an Asian American roommate. He was educating himself in the history of Asians in America, a history that was not offered in mainstream American curricula. He was learning to be a man in a culture that emasculated him and to be proud of his heritage in a culture that mocked him, surrounding himself with Asian American men whom he looked to as a family. And yet he was killed by his brothers. He was killed by Asian Americans who were just like him, people who were themselves being killed by white supremacy, by toxic masculinity, by the experience of being Asian in America.

Whether you try to assimilate into whiteness, like I did, or seek solidarity in Asian-Americanness, like Deng did; whether you're called a banana or whitewashed or FOBby; whether you're policed by white women and men or Asian women and men; whether you die by suicide or by hazing or you kill yourself slowly with alcohol and drugs and untreated mental illness, being Asian in America exacts its price. We focus on the sensational deaths—Elizabeth Shin setting herself on fire, Michael Deng's brutal beating—but there are many Elizabeths and Michaels out there, suffering in quieter, more invisible ways.

When I try to make sense of this time in my life, I think of it as akin to Stockholm syndrome, the psychological condition where victims bond emotionally to their oppressors or abusers. Some consider it a form of brainwashing, others a trauma response or survival tactic. I am not a psychiatrist; I have no idea if Stockholm syndrome is real. But it serves as a useful way to consider how minoritized people learn to survive in an oppressive society. What Du Bois called "double-consciousness," the ability to see oneself through the eyes of the white majority, is a double-edged sword. It offers the "gift of second sight" and empathy—the ability to put oneself in the shoes of another—but it can also brainwash so completely that one is trapped in the perspective of the oppressor. Trained to see oneself through a white perspective—trained to see *everything* through a white perspective—the nonwhite person ultimately loses a sense of their *own* perspective. What if, in order to survive, they must sublimate themselves completely into the worldview of their abuser?

I prefer to think of internalized racism this way because it places the blame less on the victim and more on the person or system in power. Take the example of Sandra Oh, born in Canada to Korean immigrants and one of the few actors of Asian descent to achieve mainstream success in the overwhelmingly white worlds of film and television. When Oh first moved to the United States, an agent told her, "I'm going to tell you the truth. I'm going to tell you what other people won't tell you. You're not going to work here [because you're Asian]." Oh has described the crushing shame that overcame her, a shame familiar to every person of color: "No, you're not wanted. No, you don't belong. I don't believe in you." She felt the wrenching agony of double-consciousness.

To survive, Oh did what so many of us do—she internalized the white gaze. She started seeing herself the way the outside world saw her, as a marginal character in a white production. Years later, when skimming through the script of *Killing Eve* with her agent, she couldn't figure out which part she was being considered for. It didn't cross her mind that she was being considered for the main role, the part of Eve; she had absorbed her own minoritization so thoroughly that she had preemptively disqualified herself. "[So] many years of being seen [a certain way], it deeply, deeply, deeply affects us," she said. "Oh my god! They brainwashed me! I was brainwashed!" Yet who could blame her for being "brainwashed"? In an industry infamous for rejection, Oh had protected herself by not *allowing* herself to imagine possibilities that had historically been foreclosed to her.

White supremacy is endlessly seductive. You'll think you figured out how to recognize it, how to outwit it, only to realize you've been duped all over again. And you think, *I'll do better next time.* I'll be on my guard. I won't be seduced. But then it happens again. And again. And again. Until suddenly you're like Charlie Brown and the football. You wonder why you're so gullible, so pathetic, so try-hard. You blame yourself for being so easily fooled. It's embarrassing and shameful. Well, I'm here to tell you (and to tell myself): it's not your fault. It's the system's fault. The system has brainwashed you.

I was listening to a podcast recently about people who have faked their own deaths, usually to collect insurance money or to escape prosecution. The key to successfully disappearing, an expert says, is to think like a spy. You must take on a false identity, memorize a new biography down to the tiniest fabricated details. In the language of spycraft, this is called your "legend." Your legend! You become a myth, constantly aware of how other people see you—every move, every gesture, every habit. It requires extraordinary discipline and a willingness to sever yourself completely from your family and friends. To kill your old self and replace it with a fiction. Most people can't do it.

I think I'd be very good at faking my own death. I have

no shortage of experience with putting on a false identity. I've spent my whole life being extraordinarily disciplined and seeing myself through the eyes of others. I've done it so I can collect the payout of white supremacy. I'm so good at it that it's not really faking, because I've been dying this whole time.

* * *

In my junior year, my sister joined me at Princeton. I warned her. I told her about the school's downsides, but I was also frank about its upsides. If you are an immigrant kid or a scholarship kid, you don't always have the luxury of attending the college that is the "best fit"—or of attending college at all. You go somewhere close to home, or somewhere you can afford, or somewhere you can take classes while still working and taking care of your family. Princeton's financial aid package was *five times higher* than the one offered by my sister's first-choice school. Plus, there was the brand-name recognition. I agree that the Ivy League is a stupid and meaningless "luxury" brand that is unnecessarily fetishized, but it's also a shibboleth of power. If you're not white or rich or well-connected, it is one way to open doors that would otherwise be closed to you. "I can't turn it down," my sister told me. "I can't do that to Mom and Dad."

My sister moved into my dormitory, just two floors below me. By then I was a resident adviser, which meant I got free housing and a partial meal plan in exchange for advising a group of twenty freshmen and sophomores. Many of my fellow advisers were also people of color on financial aid. For the first time, I had my own room—in fact, *two* rooms—an unexpected perk. I furnished the common area with a scavenged green armchair and broken futon and used construction paper to make knockoff Matisse cutouts that I taped to the walls. Coincidentally, I'd been assigned to the same hall that I had lived in as a first-year student. In some ways it felt like a do-over, a chance to help other students avoid the alienation I'd felt when I first arrived. I quit my dish room job but still ate at the dining hall on a regular basis. Knowing only half my meals were covered, Mrs. Williams would urge me to take extra bananas and bagels to tide me over during the day.

I took seriously my role as eonni. In my mind, I could protect my sister, keep her from making the mistakes I'd made. I was also relieved to have someone nearby who knew me and grew up in the same family. She kept me honest and confirmed that I wasn't crazy—that what I was experiencing was real. I had been convinced something was wrong with me, and I was half-expecting (and half-hoping) that my sister would love Princeton, because that would prove the problem was with *me*—that *I* was the freak who couldn't fit in. It was so much easier to blame myself than entertain the possibility that the whole system might be the problem.

But my sister didn't love it. Soon, I realized I'd recruited her into my misery. Toward the end of her first year, she told my parents she wanted to transfer, and they were distraught. What was there to hate about Princeton? How could she give up this golden ticket? My parents asked me what was going on. I was a typical older sibling, the role model, the responsible one who felt obligated to make things right. I didn't want to admit that she was struggling, that I was struggling, that this wasn't what we'd expected or wanted.

I told them we were fine—they shouldn't worry about us. Most of my phone calls home were spent listening to my parents complaining about each other, or both of them complaining about the store. The misery my sister and I felt seemed inconsequential compared to theirs. We owed it to them to suck it up.

We were all trapped in this fantasy called the American Dream, and none of us were brave enough to disavow it completely. It gave meaning to my parents' lives, it turned my sister and me into exemplars, and it glossed over the parts that were inconvenient or ugly. Karla Cornejo Villavicencio, a formerly undocumented writer who graduated from Harvard, has described the American Dream as a "pyramid scheme." She bitingly compares herself to the number one salesperson at Mary Kay, luring an endless stream of naive immigrants eager to follow in her footsteps. I felt like a con artist, too, luring my sister in, luring others in. A cheesy picture of me from the *Korea Times* was probably posted on some poor kid's fridge in Diamond Bar. Yet I didn't know how to extricate myself from the con. It was too important to keep up the charade, to save face, to avoid burdening my parents, to make them proud, to save money, to give myself a future. Under the weight of these expectations, my sister eventually dropped her plans to transfer, much to my parents' relief.

At the end of my junior year, I got a job working as an usher for baccalaureate, a formal university event before commencement that features a keynote address by some prominent alum. That year, the speaker was Senator Bill Frist, Republican of Tennessee and a future Senate majority leader. I was tasked with keeping the line of graduates and professors in full ceremonial dress moving into the chapel, a job akin to herding cats. It was a glorious day in late spring, and a group of onlookers had gathered on the flagstones to gape at the pomp and circumstance. As I stood there, chatting with a friend, both of us wearing formal black robes with tassels, an Asian woman approached me. She was middle-aged, dressed in a frumpy jacket and pants, and spoke in heavily accented English.

First, she asked me if I was Chinese. This happens often, and it doesn't bother me so much when the person is actually Chinese. I said no, but she forged ahead, undeterred.

"You're a student here?" she asked, pointing to my official robe. I nodded.

"I have a son," she said. "He's eleven years old. I want him to go here." I watched her look hungrily at the procession of dignitaries, the Gothic buildings, the manicured lawns and blooming trees. "How do I get him here? What do I do?"

At first, what I felt was annoyance. How was I to know how to get her son (who would probably be mortified if he knew what his mother was doing) into Princeton? I wasn't an admissions officer. She was a stranger. Her son was *eleven*. How tacky it was for her to accost me just because I was Asian. She was pushy and FOBby—I just wanted to get away from her.

But she wouldn't let me go, even after I gave some vague, standoffish answer.

"Is there a professor I can talk to? Who can tutor my son in English?" she asked. I blanched. I couldn't imagine giving her the name of one of my professors and asking if they could provide grammar lessons for a middle schooler. This woman had no idea how this worked! She had no idea of the hierarchy and the codes and the unspoken rules of access, yet she was trying to bulldoze her way in by approaching me. Who did she think she was?

And yet I also recognized she wasn't much different from my own mother who, had we lived near an Ivy League campus, would have likely done whatever was necessary to gain me access to its classes, facilities, teachers. I was on the other side now, *I* was the gatekeeper. I had inherited the same exclusionary thinking that had been used to keep people like me out of elite spaces. Why was I policing entry? Wasn't I supposed to "lift as I rise," not slam the door behind me?

I suddenly felt an overwhelming sadness. What I really wanted to tell this woman was: "Is this what you really want for your son? This place *looks* amazing, but it's fucked-up. Your son might not be happy. He may feel marginalized." I wanted to say: "I know I look like something out of a college brochure, but this is a costume. I'm playing a part." I wanted to warn her that it was all a con, that her son would never become the next Senator Bill Frist. In fact, neither would I. This was all a bait and switch. But I knew she wouldn't hear it. She *wanted* the fantasy I was selling in my cheap rental robe.

After some more badgering, I finally, reluctantly, gave her the email address of one of my English professors, the only Asian American professor I had. He was of mixed Japanese and white ancestry and had been born and raised in Hawaii, where his family probably went back generations. He did not study Asian American literature; he studied

Shakespeare. In many ways, he had about as little in common with this recent Chinese immigrant as anyone under the "Asian American" umbrella could have.

I wrote this professor an email, telling him he might be contacted by this woman and apologizing for any inconvenience. I didn't know how he would respond. Would he be annoyed? Perplexed? Sympathetic? Would the tenuous, unspoken, imaginary thread of Asian American solidarity hold? Did such a connection even exist?

Don't worry, he wrote back. *I totally understand.*

Chapter Eight

NEITHER/NOR

I used to swim laps in the Princeton pool for exercise. The "real" athletes worked out at the state-of-the-art sports complex across campus, but this gym was for recreational users—sorority girls and frat boys, retirees, and faculty and staff. From the outside, the building looked like a Gothic castle, with arches and turrets. Inside, the facilities were dingy and outdated. More than once, I saw cockroaches skittering down the hallways of the locker room.

One afternoon, midway through my workout, I paused at the wall to adjust my goggles when the woman in the adjacent lane turned to say something.

"Excuse me?" I said. I was wearing a swim cap, and my ears were full of water.

"Is it ni hao or konnichiwa?" she said, louder this time.

It took me a minute to register the question. *What is she asking me?* I didn't understand.

Then it dawned on me. She was asking me, "Are you Chinese or Japanese?" I did not speak Chinese or Japanese, but I'd been ni hao'd and konnichiwa'd by enough non-Asian people to know that ni hao was Mandarin for "hello," and konnichiwa was Japanese for "good day."

My stomach fell. This shit again? Even in the pool, my face covered by goggles and a cap, this woman wanted to know "what" I was. She was white and middle-aged, and she seemed extremely proud of her language skills.

I guess if I'd been a little quicker or wittier, I could have answered, "No, it's annyeonghaseyo" and watched her struggle to decode my words. Or I could have said, "Actually, it's hello" and swum away. But I didn't. Instead, I blurted out the first thing I could think of.

"It's neither," I said.

The woman looked surprised, then embarrassed. I'm sure she heard the edge in my voice.

"Oh," she finally said, laughing awkwardly. "Well, you know us ignorant Westerners."

She pushed off from the wall before I could say anything else. I stared at her as she swam away, speechless. An "ignorant Westerner"? I wanted to shout after her. "I was born here! Didn't you notice I don't have an accent? I'm a Westerner, too!"

But the exchange was over. She'd had the last word (as well as the first!).

I got out of the pool feeling nauseated. I'd been trying to answer this question since I was *four years old.* What could I have done differently or said instead? I had tried to make myself legible to this woman—I was neither Chinese nor Japanese—and had only succeeded in worsening the misunderstanding. When I didn't respond the way the woman wanted or expected, she simply repeated the terms of our encounter. In this role-play, she was the "ignorant Westerner" and I was—what? The inscrutable Oriental? She had conscripted me into a role I did not want to play.

At the time, I was taking my first literary theory class, and we'd been reading *Black Skin, White Masks* by Frantz Fanon. Fanon was a major figure of the African diaspora, born in the French colony of Martinique in the Caribbean. He wrote extensively about the psychological and political impact of European conquest and racism on the postcolonial subject. In a famous essay, he describes the experience of being a Black man in white spaces.

"Look, a Negro!" Fanon hears as he walks down the street. A white child is pointing Fanon out to his mother: "*Maman*, I'm scared . . . *Maman*, the Negro is going to eat me."

For Fanon, this moment is an act of supreme annihilation. To this child, he isn't human. He's a monster, a boogeyman, a cannibal. Fanon is drenched in "shame and self-contempt. Nausea."

Yet versions of this phrase haunt Fanon even in his interactions with supposedly enlightened white adults. Sometimes it takes the form of paternalism—"We have a Senegalese history teacher. He's very intelligent." Sometimes it takes the form of fetishization—"Look how handsome that Negro is"—or the form of affiliation—"I'd like you to meet my black friend." But always, always, lurking beneath, is the white framing of Blackness as inherently inferior and exotic and other. These white intellectuals may not be as blunt as the child—"Look! A Negro!"—but they simply dress up their objectification in backhanded praise. "Look! A Negro who is articulate and intelligent!" "Look! A Negro who is handsome!" "Look! A Negro who is friendly!"

Fanon's analysis of racial minoritization helped me start to understand what had happened in the pool. From beginning to end, my encounter had unfolded within the parameters of whiteness. The terms of the encounter were set by the white woman, and they were set without my consent. She did not call me "a Negro" or even "oriental." She did not use a racial epithet. She saw herself as an enlightened and worldly person, an intellectual (I can speak Chinese! I can speak Japanese!). Yet I felt the familiar nausea of dehumanization nonetheless. "Look! An Oriental!"

Human beings are social creatures—we crave connection and belonging. Without it, we feel lost or unworthy or invisible. Yet what happens when human connection is constantly being thwarted? When even quotidien, "friendly" exchanges are doomed to fail because one party *still* can't see the other as fully human? I am not talking about cartoon examples of racism. I am talking about subtler forms of dehumanization that lurk in fetishization, exoticization, and paternalism. Each moment of disconnection leaves its victim with a spasm of shame, a flicker of self-contempt, and existential nausea. We absorb this in our bodies; we see ourselves as dishonorable, unworthy of connection.

Yet isn't that, ironically, the ultimate proof of our humanity? That the act of being dehumanized and disconnected fills *us* with shame? That we so desperately desire connection that we blame *ourselves* for the failed exchange?*

* * *

---

* In her book *Citizen: An American Lyric*, Claudia Rankine, citing Judith Butler, notes that what makes us most human—our openness and addressability—is the very thing racists exploit to dehumanize us.

James Baldwin famously said, "To be a Negro in this country and to be relatively conscious is to be in a state of rage almost all of the time."

I would argue that to be an Asian person in this country and to be relatively conscious is to be in a state of shame almost all of the time.

Over and over, I've been told that East Asian societies are "shame prone," a by-product of its collectivist nature. In contrast, American society is valorized as rugged and individualistic. For a long time, I accepted this simplistic binary. I believed that my struggles with shame and worthiness could be traced to the failings and idiosyncrasies of my parents' culture, passed down to me.

"Your mother always shamed you," a white therapist once told me. "You've struggled with feelings of inadequacy and insufficiency because that is your cultural heritage."

I used to buy this line of reasoning. Didn't my Asian American friends and I always joke about it? How our parents were reluctant to affirm and compliment? How they emphasized modesty and humility? How bringing home a 98 wasn't enough because where were the other two points? I mean, of course we were all overachievers, desperate for parental approval that would never come.

But I am American as much as I am Korean, born in this country and acculturated to its values. And I think it is far too easy to blame my parents for all the ways in which I have been fucked up. Sure, they fucked me up, but so did white supremacy. It is not just Korean and Confucian values that are to blame for my unending feelings of shame. It is the white American values I am bathed in every single day of my life.

To live as a minoritized, nonwhite person in this country is to exist in a perpetual state of shame. It is to be told every day: "You will never belong. You will never be enough. You will never be American—by which, we mean you will never be white."

Take the incarceration of Japanese Americans in concentration camps during World War II, an act of public shaming on a historical scale. Under Executive Order 9066, FDR authorized the wholesale removal of over a hundred thousand people of Japanese descent from the West Coast, deeming them a threat to national security. Families lost their homes, their businesses, their civil rights. Many camp survivors refused to talk about the experience in the years after, retreating into silence and denial. Scholars have pointed to the cultural aspects to this response: issei and nisei (first- and second-generation Japanese Americans) felt a collective shame at their internment and responded by embracing Japanese values of gaman ("to endure or persevere with dignity") and shikata ga nai ("it can't be undone") as a way to cope.

But white American culture was responsible for seeding that racial shame, cultivating it, ritualizing it, and weaponizing it. It publicly expelled Japanese Americans from the American civic body and dehumanized them, calling them "Japs" and "enemy aliens." No wonder camp survivors felt marked; no wonder they wanted to forget about it and move on.

On a smaller scale, microaggressions are subtle acts of shaming. Individually, they may not seem that bad. You flinch inwardly and move on. But compounded day after day, time after time, they erode your self-worth and dignity. Claudia Rankine describes how relentless these moments are, like being constantly under attack. You're ambushed while swimming laps or eating lunch or sitting in class. You feel wounded and shamed; a little part of you dies. You have to take a moment to gather yourself, to bandage the wound or brush it off as superficial. Otherwise, how can you survive in this world? If every microaggression undid you, you'd die.

When I was a child, my mother always used to say to me, "You are not white. You'll have to work twice as hard and be twice as good in order to get half as far." A lot of BIPOC kids have heard something similar from their parents. For my mother, it was a way of preparing me for the hurdles I'd face. She was setting expectations and even motivating me: look, it won't be easy for you, so you better work hard and be prepared for disappointment.

I *hated* hearing this when I was younger. To my childhood ears, it sounded like my mother was telling me to make my dreams smaller. Warning me not to get too greedy or too cocky. Shaming me.

"You're so negative," I would yell at her. "You don't believe in me." I assumed she was telling me I was unworthy, when really, it was white supremacy that was telling me I was unworthy. My mother was simply the messenger.

As I got older, I had to admit that my mother was right. I *would* have to work twice as hard and be twice as good to get half as far. But in my mind, I'd already developed what I thought was an ingenious strategy around this. I would just work *ten times harder* and be *ten times as good*, and in that way I'd somehow compensate for my racial disadvantages. I could exorcise feelings of shame through superhuman effort and achievement, clinging to the fantasy of meritocracy.

I'm reminded of how W. E. B. Du Bois responded to

his own childhood experience of racial exclusion. Du Bois grew up in an integrated community in New England and attended school with white children. Exchanging visiting cards one day, he presented a card to a new white girl in class. The girl refused the card—refused it "peremptorily, with a glance"—and Du Bois felt "the shadow," the veil that separates Black America from white America. He is Black. He will never belong. He can only peer through the veil at a whiteness forbidden to him.

Du Bois's response is to sneer at the white world beyond the veil, to reject its rejection of him. He finds solace in beating his white classmates on exams or in races, or even beating "their stringy heads." But as he gets older, this isn't enough. He wants the "dazzling opportunities" offered to those on the white side of the veil. He ends up being the first Black person to earn a PhD from Harvard University. Some of his Black peers resort to other methods of survival within systemic racism—they fall into "sycophancy" toward whiteness, or hatred of the white world, or despair at their plight. But Du Bois fights back in what he believes is a more productive way. He believes education will be the armor that shields him from white supremacy's vilification of Blackness. "I sit with Shakespeare and he winces not," Du Bois writes. "Across the color line I move arm in arm with Balzac and Dumas."

I thought I could be like Du Bois. I thought I could beat white people at their own game. I would out-elite the elite and seize the "dazzling opportunities" of whiteness. At Princeton, I threw myself into classes and extracurriculars, jamming my days with activity so I didn't have time to think or feel. I was one of those nerds who *never* missed lecture or precept, even if I was hungover or unprepared, because I knew how dearly those courses cost in tuition dollars and parental sacrifice. Overachievement became my antidote to the shame of not being enough. If Du Bois could do it, so could I. I'd show white people. I'd be so fucking amazing that they couldn't help but recognize my worthiness.

It didn't work. And it didn't work for Du Bois, either. There's a terrible joke that goes, "What do you call a Black man with a PhD? A n—r." No matter what Du Bois achieved, no matter how high he went, he could be cut down in a split second by a slur. And it wasn't just the white world that demeaned him. Marcus Garvey, the charismatic Black Nationalist and Pan-Africanist, called Du Bois a "white man's n—r," someone who was ashamed of his Blackness. The shame rained down from all sides. He was too white or not white enough. Too uppity or too sycophantic. A tool of racial uplift or a sellout.

How painfully I recognize this desperate dance to outdo whiteness, or reject whiteness, or abject oneself to whiteness. To attack those who are too Black or not Black enough. Too Asian or not Asian enough. Even invoking Du Bois here fills me with shame, because who am I, a Korean American woman living in the twenty-first century, to see myself in a Black man living at the height of Jim Crow? I'm acutely aware that the Black experience is different from the Asian experience, that the racial trauma Du Bois faced cannot be compared to my own. How dare I even complain? Cathy Park Hong writes, "I am a dog cone of shame. I am a urinal cake of shame. . . . I am pure incinerating shame." To be an Asian person in this country and to be relatively conscious is to be in a state of shame almost all of the time.

* * *

If there's a way out of this abyss of shame, perhaps it's through empathy. That's what Brené Brown, the author and clinical social worker, argues. Although Brown doesn't talk specifically about racial shame, she defines shame broadly as the fear of disconnection. A racist joke or an ignorant comment inspires racial shame in a person by severing them from others and casting them in a shadow. The best antidote to shame, then, is empathy, which restores a sense of connectedness and belonging. Confiding your experience in a friend, reading about a similar experience in a book or magazine, taking a class with fellow people of color—all of these can make you feel less alone. Racial shame flourishes in a white supremacist system intent on separating people of color from one another. The best way to counteract it is to connect with those who have also felt its sting.*

Ironically, Princeton is where I first recognized the brainwashing of white supremacy and sought solidarity with other Asian Americans and people of color who felt marginalized. I found my way to these communities of color established by previous generations of students on campus—spaces like the Third World Center, founded by Black activists in the 1970s to support the growing number of Black and brown students arriving on campus (among them Sonia Sotomayor and Michelle Obama, who both served on its student governance board) and the community of advisers at the residential colleges, who acted as

---

* According to Brown, "If we can share our story with someone who responds with empathy and understanding, shame can't survive." See her TED Talk, "Listening to Shame." Thank you to MC for introducing me to Brown's work.

resources and sounding boards for students of color on campus. Joining these communities was my first step out of the shadow of racial shame.

Another was learning more about the history of Asian American identity. This was easier said than done on a campus where Asian American studies classes weren't offered and ethnic studies of any sort were considered lacking in rigor. At the end of my freshman year, a group of juniors and seniors staged a thirty-six-hour sit-in in the president's office to demand the establishment of a Latino Studies and Asian American Studies program, and the administration responded with vague assurances of support but little action. (It would take until 2018, more than *twenty years later*, for the university to officially create a program in Asian American Studies.) I ended up gleaning information from issues of *A. Magazine* and *Yolk*, which somehow made their way into my campus mailbox, and through Elaine Kim's book *Asian American Literature*, which my mother had bought for me after reading an interview with the author in the Korean newspaper.

I was surprised by what I learned. I hadn't known that the term "Asian American" originated as a radical act of self-determination. Coined in the late 1960s by Yuji Ichioka and Emma Gee, student activists at Berkeley, "Asian American" was envisioned as a way to unify the diverse ethnicities, languages, and cultures that comprised Asia into a distinct racial and sociopolitical identity. Inspired by the Black Power and Black Pride movements, Asian American students at Berkeley and San Francisco State rejected "oriental" stereotypes that had been used to paint them as docile and pitted them against other racial groups. Instead, they stood in solidarity with their colleagues of color against white supremacy and imperialism, forming a multiracial coalition called the Third World Liberation Front. Three thousand miles away, students at Princeton created their own Third World Coalition, pressing successfully for the creation of the Third World Center.

Today, the term Asian American has become detached from its radical political origins and has morphed into a generic demographic category on census forms, marketing questionnaires, and surveys. And like all racial constructions, even self-determined ones, "Asian American" is an imperfect term, accused of being both overly broad and absurdly simplistic. A second-generation Korean American woman like me, who was raised in predominantly white spaces in a middle-class household in Los Angeles, has a vastly different experience from that of a Hmong refugee who lives in a predominantly Hmong agricultural community in Minnesota or a fifth-generation American of Filipino, Kānaka Maoli, and Japanese descent living in Hawaii. Different Asian American ethnic groups vote differently (Vietnamese Americans tend to lean Republican; Indian Americans tend to lean Democratic), just as different Latinx ethnic groups vote differently (Puerto Ricans lean Democratic; Cuban Americans lean Republican). Asian Americans are among the very wealthiest and the very poorest of Americans. There is no common language or religion or history—just a collection of people from disparate corners of Asia, loosely held together by political expediency and a shared experience of discrimination.

At its worst, "Asian American" is simply an updated euphemism for "Oriental," a flabby category that emerges

from the same absurd white supremacist logic as the iden-
tifier "Negro." Honestly, American racial categories have
never made any sense, constructed as they are around
whiteness and implying monolithic identities. They origi-
nate in pseudoscientific racial taxonomies used by European colonizers to justify the conquest and subjugation of
non-European people, whose phenotypic differences were a
mark, they believed, of their racial inferiority and degenera-
tion. Someone born in Korea doesn't think of themselves as
"Asian"—they identify as "Korean." Someone born in Nige-
ria doesn't think of themselves as "Black"—they identify as,
say, Igbo.* Yet the minute all of us step into the American
racial imaginary, we are marked as "not-white."

The truth is that whatever you think about these racial
classifications, this is the way the government, marketers,
and large portions of the American public will categorize
you. The first Asian American activists recognized this and
saw an opportunity to take the racial identity foisted upon
them, redefine it, and use it to build coalitions and power.
As diluted as the term "Asian American" has become today,
as fragmented the community and fractious its members, I
still believe in its original promise.

"What about us?" I sometimes hear Asian Americans or
other non-Black minority groups complain. Black issues, it's
suggested, suck up all the available oxygen. When Americans

---

* The term Latinx truly makes no sense. On bureaucratic forms, the box for
"Latinx" is separate from the box for "Black," but there are Latinx people
with African and Indigenous heritage, as well as Latinx people who have 100
percent European ancestry. There's been recent discussion of how some members of the Latinx community, like the Irish, the Italian, and the Eastern European Jews before them, have fled into whiteness.

talk about racism in the United States, they usually mean anti-Black racism. Black Lives Matter gets all the headlines, some Asian Americans argue, and there is no shortage of prominent Black figures. This resentment, I'm convinced, emerges from our collective brainwashing by white supremacy, which tells us that there's only a certain amount of bandwidth available in the American consciousness to deal with racial oppression—and that bandwidth has already been claimed by Black people. We need to refuse this culture of scarcity—a culture, I argue, that is foundational to white supremacy. How about we take more space from the dominant culture instead of trying to steal it from other minority cultures? How about we refuse to compete for whiteness?

Like the original members of the Third World Liberation Front, I believe that Asian Americans should advocate for Asian American issues while also supporting their Black allies and fighting anti-Black racism. It's not either/or. That's a con perpetrated by the dominant culture. The Asian American, Yellow Power, and AZN Pride movements would not exist without the political, social, and cultural groundwork laid by Black Americans. If we turn against our Black allies, we undermine our own efforts. If we dishonor them, we dishonor ourselves. We self-sabotage our collective efforts to dismantle white supremacy.

I'm grateful to allies like Gabrielle Union, who protested on the set of *America's Got Talent* when Jay Leno cracked a joke about Korean people eating dogs. The joke wasn't at Black people's expense, but in some ways it *was*. Leno was cracking a white supremacist joke, a joke that Asian people are barbaric and inhuman and can be mocked with impunity. It's the same logic behind stereotypes of Black inhumanity—denigrate this racial other to endorse white-ness, reduce them to a laughingstock. When an Asian per-son laughs at an anti-Black joke, or a Black person laughs at an anti-Asian joke, the person who actually gets the last laugh is the white supremacist. Justice isn't BIPOC folks feuding with one another for the same small piece of pie. It's realizing that we all deserve more of the whole damn pie.*

---

* Leno eventually apologized for his history of anti-Asian jokes after the murders of six women of Asian descent in Atlanta in March 2021. Too bad it took a mass shooting for him to realize he's racist.

Chapter Nine

ORIENTALISM

In 1996, I won a scholarship to travel in the summer between my sophomore and junior years in college. Past recipients had used the money to go rock climbing at national parks, or to visit every Major League baseball stadium in the country. I wanted to visit English gardens. I'd just finished reading George Eliot's *Middlemarch* and was an enormous Anglophile. When I got the award, I couldn't believe my luck. The previous summer I'd spent folding sweaters at Express in the Century City Mall. Now I'd get to travel through England to live out a Jane Austen fantasy.

I quickly figured out that England was like nothing I'd seen in books or movies. I was a nineteen-year-old Asian girl traveling alone with three changes of clothes and a daily allowance of thirty pounds, which I spent on Cadbury Fruit & Nut bars from Underground vending machines. The racial landscape was different. "Asian" meant South Asian, not East Asian, though the tone of derision was the same. Everyone thought I was Japanese. I tried explaining that I was American but got puzzled looks and sometimes hostility in return (people hated Americans; I contemplated saying I was Canadian). I was harassed. A lot.

Occasionally, I'd stay in bed-and-breakfasts when there was no hostel nearby. I did that on Guernsey, a channel island between England and France, which is how I somehow got into a conversation with a group of middle-aged white guys while eating breakfast. They were the British version of bros (blokes?), joking with one another and bragging about their exploits. They offered to drive me to the airport to catch my flight, and for some stupid reason (probably that I was broke and didn't want to pay taxi fare), I said OK. After they dropped me off, they asked for my college mailing address, so they could "keep in touch." And again, for some stupid reason (I didn't want to be rude; I was grateful for the ride), I said OK.*

I forgot about this incident until a few months later, when I got a letter in my dorm mailbox. It was from one of the men I'd met on Guernsey. His name was Archie and he was balding and paunchy and looked like Homer Simpson. In several excruciatingly handwritten pages, Archie professed his admiration of my "oriental" beauty and expressed interest in being pen pals or maybe something more (hint hint). He enclosed several photos of various propeller planes (he was a recreational pilot). In one photo, he posed in a cockpit in a pilot's uniform, staring broodingly at the camera.

I was taken aback. First of all, I was offended. I'm no supermodel, but I'm also no troll. The fact that Archie thought he had a chance with me—someone half his age,

---

* Note to my daughter and every other young woman who is reading this: DO NOT EVER DO THIS. This is so dangerous and stupid, and I can't believe I wasn't kidnapped or raped or killed.

with no common interests—was frankly insulting. I couldn't care less about planes, but he'd taken my politeness as an invitation to tell me all about himself and his interests. Any woman can relate to this. Smiling and being polite to a guy does not mean we want to sleep with him. Don't flatter yourself.

I also knew that if I were a white girl, Archie wouldn't have written to me. He would have assumed that I was out of his league. A white girl had choices; a white girl could get any guy she wanted. But I was Asian, so he thought he had a chance. He probably had friends who went to Thailand and the Philippines on sex tours, and I'm sure he saw older British dudes with their younger, Asian mail-order brides.

I was experiencing firsthand the dehumanization that undergirds yellow fever, otherwise known as the "Asian fetish." Most commonly referring to white men who are exclusively attracted to Asian women, the Asian fetish taps into all the racial stereotypes that adhere to Asian women— that we're submissive, hypersexual, and exotic. The white man, in contrast, is dominant and hypermasculine. I call it Orientalism Gone Wild, a form of sexual role-play that re-creates the original racial and power dynamics of European colonialism. Like my exchange with the white lady in the pool, I was supposed to welcome this attention with delight. In this case, I was also supposed to spread my legs.

The poet Marianne Chan illustrates this vividly in her description of a rehearsal for the Filipino festival Sinulog, which commemorates the coming of the Spaniards and the introduction of Christianity to the Philippines. Taking place in Lansing, Michigan, the rehearsal eerily re-creates the racial and power dynamics of European colonialism, with "all the Filipina wives" playing native dancers and their white husbands "playing conquistadors, because what were / conquistadors if not small-town men with beer breath." In another poem, Chan recalls "the white husband / of my parents' friend" who tells her he "wanted to own a Filipino" and proudly shows her photos of his bikini-clad wife. He thinks he's flaunting his masculinity, but Chan just sees a pathetic and delusional middle-aged white man.

Orientalist fantasies are everywhere. In my sophomore year of college, I went to see my first Broadway musical, *Miss Saigon*, paying twenty dollars for a subsidized ticket and round-trip bus fare from my dorm to midtown Manhattan. The musical had already faced controversy over white male actors being cast in yellowface for its Eurasian roles, but I'd set aside my misgivings in my excitement to see Lea Salonga, the star of the show and the first woman of Asian descent to win a Tony Award. Over the course of the performance, that excitement turned to disgust. While I loved hearing Salonga sing, I *hated* the role she was given—a Vietnamese bar girl, part of a lurid landscape of brothels frequented by white American soldiers, one of whom fucks, impregnates, and then deserts her, taking her child back to America. She is drenched in shame and self-contempt; the musical ends with her suicide. I bitched to my friend Sandhya about the musical the entire bus ride back to campus. I couldn't understand why people thought it was a romance. It was white supremacist propaganda.

Miss Saigon was based on Puccini's opera *Madama Butterfly*, itself an orientalist fantasy featuring a white American soldier and his Asian (in this case Japanese) lover, whom he fucks, impregnates, and leaves, taking her child with him. In both *Miss Saigon* and *Madama Butterfly*, the women kill themselves at the end. The Asian woman *always* dies. Her sexual exploitation and dishonor and death are necessary to the white male colonialist fantasy. She becomes an allegory for her country—desired, pillaged, then abandoned when no longer useful. Meanwhile, the white man always gets to live. He always gets to tell the story, turning it into a tragic romance and making himself its hero.

You can dismiss these stories as outdated and categorize Archie as an extreme example of white male entitlement/ delusion, but his behavior and attitude exist in all sorts of subtler and more insidious ways. In the same way there are whisper networks among women about sketchy men, there are whisper networks among Asian women about men with yellow fever. And it's not just older white guys like Woody Allen or Nicolas Cage or your lechy white-haired boss who winks at you. It's young white guys, too. I call them Jasons. Some of them major in East Asian Studies and brag about how they are fluent in Mandarin and taught English in Korea or whatever. Some of them are really into Japanese martial arts and strut around campus looking like the Karate Kid. Some like to rhapsodize over "authentic" Asian food and tattoo Chinese characters on their biceps, and some even bring home an Asian girlfriend or wife.

Go to Google and type "Asian women" in the search bar. The top hits are always porn sites or mail-order bride sites or sex tourism sites. As the tech scholar Chris Gilliard has pointed out, Google isn't an information search engine. It's an ideological search engine. It reproduces and amplifies the belief system of its users, its content creators, the entire digital world. And that belief system is patriarchal and white supremacist. If you want to learn more about Asian women, you will discover that the most "relevant" things to know about us is that we are sexual fetish objects. Type in "Korean women" or "Filipina women" or "Vietnamese women" or "Thai women"—it doesn't matter. See what comes up. I dare you.

* * *

In March 2021, a white gunman killed eight people in Atlanta, six of them women of Asian descent. The victims worked at massage parlors and spas; they were mothers and grandmothers, wives and sisters and daughters. Four of them were Korean women, ranging in age from fifty-one to seventy-four. In the aftermath, a police spokesperson said the killer was having a "bad day" and that he was motivated by a "sex addiction," not racism. Later, I heard FBI director Christopher Wray declare on the radio that it did not appear the shootings were racially motivated.

I started pounding on the steering wheel in my car. For more than a year, I'd been reading about incidents of anti-Asian harassment around the country, incidents that had mostly gone unnoticed by the general public. Now, here was an episode of anti-Asian hate that was so spectacular and newsworthy it could not be denied. And yet law enforcement still reported that race was not a factor. The killer was a white man, the police spokesperson was a white man, the FBI director was a white man. They were all telling me to ignore what I knew in my gut as a woman of Asian descent living in a white supremacist society. If killing six Asian women wasn't about anti-Asian and misogynist hate, then what was it about?

Men want to fuck us *and* kill us. Archies, Jasons, the Atlanta shooter—they are all trafficking in white supremacist fantasies, fantasies built on a toxic mix of racism and misogyny. Orientalism and anti-Asian hate are not contradictory; they are two halves of the same coin. They both serve to dehumanize and dishonor Asian women. The white guy who yells "me love you long time" is not interested in me as a human being. I'm just an accessory to his distorted fantasy of white male domination. I have had to stave off these advances my entire life, and let me tell you, they are *not* a compliment. They are a threat. If I reject these men, who knows what they will do? Kill me? Assault me? Blame me for seducing them?

When I opened that letter from Archie twenty-five years ago, I wasn't just offended by his "romantic" overtures. I was low-key scared. Standing outside the mailroom, clutching the handwritten pages and sheaf of photos, I realized that Archie knew my address. An ocean separated us, but he was a pilot and could easily fly over from England. What if he showed up on my doorstep?

As I stood there, one of my dorm's faculty advisers, a middle-aged white man, walked by and, seeing the look on my face, asked me what was wrong. I told him what had happened, showing him the stack of pictures and the handwritten letter. "What should I do?" I asked him. "Should I be concerned?" The professor laughed awkwardly, looking as if he wanted to run away. "I'm sure he's harmless," he said. "You shouldn't be scared of him—you should feel sorry for him. Imagine how he must feel."

He's harmless. You shouldn't be scared. Imagine how he must feel.

Thankfully, I never heard from Archie again. I felt a little better when I moved to a different dorm room the following year, and better yet when I graduated and left the campus for good.

Chapter Ten

BOOGEYMEN

When I graduated college in 1998, my parents took me to Korea as a graduation gift. I hadn't visited the country since I was a toddler, and my parents hadn't been back since the early 1980s. My sister would not be joining us because she was retaking organic chemistry at a local community college over the summer. Meanwhile, I had not spent this much time alone with my parents since I left for college. Without the buffer of my sister or three thousand miles of distance, I worried I might kill them and/or myself.

The fact we were even taking a vacation was surreal. Since buying Pioneer Chicken, my parents hadn't had the time or money to go on vacation. But after years of unsuccessfully trying to unload their business, my parents had found a buyer, a South Asian entrepreneur who owned a string of Subway franchises. The spring of my senior year, they sold their store for less than half of what they'd originally paid for it. All three of us were now at loose ends.

We flew from Los Angeles to Seoul, a trip that took more than thirteen hours. My parents were shocked by how dramatically the country had changed. The last time they'd visited, South Korea was still under military rule and just beginning its economic ascent. Fifteen years later, the country had a democratically elected president and was an economic juggernaut, exporting semiconductors, electronics, automobiles, and more. In a single generation, it had gone from one of the poorest countries in the world to one of the most developed. My parents couldn't get over how modern Seoul was, how crowded and technologically advanced it was. They felt like they were stepping into an alternate reality.

My parents signed us up for a ten-day sightseeing tour, most of which was spent riding on a motor coach. I was the youngest person on the bus by at least three decades. The tour guide did not speak English; I did not speak Korean. At first, my parents tried to translate the tour guide's commentary for me, but they soon gave up and left me alone. I read Zadie Smith's *White Teeth* and sulked while the rest of the bus sang karaoke. My parents bickered as usual—my dad complained that my mom talked too much, my mom grumbled that my dad walked too slow.

We visited Seoraksan on the tour, a famous mountain twenty miles south of the North Korean border, near the port city of Sokcho. Just days before our arrival, a North Korean spy submarine had been discovered by local fishermen in the waters nearby, tangled in a drift net. Inside the submarine were the bodies of nine soldiers, who had committed murder/suicide rather than surrender to South Korean forces. The newspapers were full of stories about the gruesome discovery, reviving fears that North Korean spies might be lurking undetected in the area. Our tour guide assured us that Seoraksan was safe, but my mother was visibly on edge. The mountain was crowded with tourists and shrouded in a fog so thick you could barely see your own feet. Anyone could be hiding in our midst.

My mother had grown up in a rural village near the southwest coast of the peninsula, and though she hadn't escaped across the border like my father had, her experience of the war was marked by constant fear and insecurity. At night, North Korean sympathizers would slip down from their hiding places in the mountains and lurk outside her home, calling her name. My mother was something of a local celebrity, because her father had been an "old man" (in his forties) when she was born. "Meng-Soon! Meng-Soon!" the men would cry. "We're starving! Give us food!" My mother was only six or seven years old, but in her mind, they were real-life boogeymen, ready to snatch her away. She dreaded nightfall and desperately prayed for rain because those were the only times when the men did not come.

My mother knew she was lucky; she saw less fortunate children everywhere—refugees, orphans, amputees. At any moment, she knew she, too, could be hurt or killed. Bombs fell at night, leaving craters in the nearby rice paddies. A group of children from her village went to collect firewood and were blown up when they stumbled upon an undetonated shell. Her half brother was struck in the mouth with shrapnel, lost all his teeth, and sustained brain damage. During school, gunfights erupted outside between police and North Korean sympathizers, forcing the children to dive under their desks for protection. On the way home, she passed piles of corpses, the bodies of suspected Communists who had been shot to death and left to rot in a ditch.

I didn't know any of this when we were on our trip. I just thought my mother seemed more agitated than usual. The next day, our tour group visited the DMZ (Demilitarized Zone), the 160-mile border separating North Korea and South Korea. I won't lie; it was freaky. Despite its name, the DMZ is one of the most highly militarized zones in the world, a no-man's-land heavily patrolled by armed troops on both sides of the demarcation line. Bill Clinton has called it "the scariest place on earth." We boarded a shuttle at Camp Bonifas, the United Nations command post, driving silently past rice paddies that had once been studded with land mines, arriving at Panmunjom, the border village that led to the Joint Security Area. Our USO guide was a young white American soldier in a crew cut and fatigues. He had clearly memorized his script, barking out facts and history with hardly a pause for breath. We stuck close to him as we entered the bright blue conference building where delegations from the North and the South met for talks. All around us were ROK soldiers in uniforms and helmets, grim and unsmiling as they guarded the perimeter. At the other end of the building, through a closed door, was North Korea.

"Can you hear that?" our guide asked once we were back outside. "That's the sound of North Korean propaganda being played over loudspeakers across the border." He pointed to a cluster of buildings in the distance. "Those houses are just stage sets," he said. "No one lives there—it's all a facade. We call it Propaganda Village."

On the way back to Camp Bonifas, we stopped at a memorial park with exhibits depicting North Korean artillery, clothing, and other artifacts, all of it described as shoddy and inferior. I wondered if North Korea had similar exhibits of shoddy, inferior South Korean artifacts on the other side. There were descriptions of how malnourished North Koreans were, how they'd endured a period of famine in which hundreds of thousands of citizens died of starvation, how the average North Korean was inches shorter and many pounds lighter than the average South Korean. To me, North Korea seemed sad and pathetic, not scary. My mother, on the other hand, could barely stand to read the descriptions. She shook her head. "Such a tragedy," she said. "So much suffering."

I assumed my mother's anxiety would lift once we returned to Los Angeles. But to my chagrin, it got worse. At LAX, on the pedestrian walkway to baggage claim, a Korean man who had been on our flight asked my mother for directions to the corner of Western and Olympic in Koreatown. He was dressed in a suit like a businessman and carried a small suitcase. I thought it was an innocent question, but as soon as he left, my mother turned to me and said, "He's a spy. He's checking to see if I'm actually from the area and know the streets in Koreatown." I thought she was joking, but she kept looking over her shoulder while we waited for our luggage at the carousel and then got into the cab line. During the car ride home, my father and I started arguing with her.

"Why would someone follow you all the way from Korea?" we asked. "Why are you even worth following?"

"I don't know!" my mother said. She admitted that she had tried to mail her friend a letter while we were on our trip, but the post office clerk found the American address suspicious and asked her a bunch of questions. She was sure "they" had opened it and read the contents.

"Why on earth would anyone want to read your letter?" I asked. "What were you writing about?"

"Nothing!" my mom said. "Just normal stuff."

"If there was nothing in your letter, why would they still be following you?"

"Maybe they think *I'm* a spy," she said.

"*You*, a *spy*?" I started laughing. "Who are you spying for?? North Korea? The United States? South Korea? That's ridiculous! What side are you supposed to be on?"

"I don't know!" my mom said.

"You're being paranoid," my dad said. "No one is following you. You're not that important."

My mother glared at us. Over the next week, she stuck to her story but otherwise acted normal. She still got up each day, still went to the YMCA, still went to Mass. I was hopeful the delusion had passed. But a week later, my mother told us that someone had followed her home from church.

"I saw him in my rearview mirror," she said. "He was driving right behind me the entire time."

"Oh my God, Mom," I said. "I'm sure it was a coincidence!"

"No—it wasn't a coincidence. It was an Asian man. Maybe it was the same person who stopped me at the airport. He drove away when I pulled into the driveway."

This is it, I said to myself. My mother has officially gone off the deep end. My dad teased her, trying to make her see the absurdity of her beliefs, the sheer impossibility that someone would fly *all the way from Korea* to shadow her—why? Because she'd mailed a letter?

My mother could not be reasoned with. In her mind, *we* were the ones who were in denial. She was so insistent that

I started to wonder if maybe she was right. What if people actually *were* following her? We knew North Korean agents routinely infiltrated South Korea. They'd kidnapped fishermen, high school students, even a famous film actress who North Korean dictator Kim Jong Il had become enamored with. One former North Korean spy claimed there were "hundreds" of agents in the United States working to recruit Korean Americans sympathetic to the North Korean cause. What if they were trying to kidnap or recruit my mother?

Holy shit, I thought. Maybe my mother *was* a spy. She'd always been secretive about her past. She spoke Korean and English fluently, and she'd spoken German at one point as well. She knew how to bind a wound, resuscitate patients, start an IV. She was in excellent physical shape, and she could slip into spaces without arousing suspicion. Who better than her to be a double agent? What if she were a Korean Jason Bourne?

After days of going back and forth, wondering whether we needed to go to the FBI, the CIA, or the ER, my mother made an announcement.

"The man left," she told us. "He must have figured out I'm not a spy. I haven't seen him since. It's such a relief!"

My dad and I looked at each other. "There was never anyone following you—" I started.

"He's gone," my mom said. "They must have gotten me mixed up with the wrong person."

"You need to get your head checked," my dad said. "You're crazy."

"You need to get *your* head checked," my mom said.

She looked around, then raised her voice in case "they" were listening.

"I am not a spy," she said. "I did nothing wrong."

* * *

For years, I'd assumed my father was the one who bore greater trauma from the Korean War. My mother hadn't made a harrowing escape across the border, hadn't been thrown in jail, hadn't experienced starvation. Compared to my father, her experience of the war seemed relatively cushy. When she did speak of it, she always fixated on the disembodied voices outside her home. I used to roll my eyes, dismissing her fears as the overblown nightmares of a child. A minor ghost story. Nothing like my father's experience, which was gritty and suspenseful and real.

"My mom is crazy," I'd often tell people. "You won't believe the latest thing she said/did/bought." But this was on a whole different level. I tried to intellectualize the incident, analyzing it the way I would analyze a novel or poem. Maybe the stress of my mother's Korean homecoming, plus the spy submarine incident and the visit to the DMZ, had triggered a psychotic break in my mom. The trauma of the Korean War had never fully been resolved. Returning to the spot where the country had been cleaved in two had cleaved something inside her own mind, causing her anxiety to bloom into paranoia.

Or maybe my mother was experiencing an identity crisis. She'd now spent as much time living in America as she had living in Korea; she no longer recognized this new, shiny country as her homeland. If anything, she felt like more of a foreigner in Korea than she did in the United States. Her pre-occupation with spies—North Korean spies, secret agents, sympathizers—was a manifestation of her own in-between status. She felt like a traitor, a woman without a country.

Or maybe this was really about han, that uniquely Korean persecution complex. It flared up in times of stress, subsided in times of peace. I'd seen it before, when she worried that she'd be held up at gunpoint at the store; when she was certain I'd fall in with the "wrong" crowd. There were *always* boogeymen out there, ready to take you and your family down.

Still, I felt a weird wobble of uncertainty. The scaffold of explanations I'd constructed wasn't holding. What if the truth was that my mother *was* being watched, and her behavior was the logical consequence of this surveillance? In college, I had learned about the panopticon, a system of modern social control first designed by English philosopher Jeremy Bentham and later developed by the French theorist Michel Foucault. Originating in eighteen-century prison design, the panopticon, or all-seeing eye, allowed a single guard in a central tower to observe an entire rotunda filled with inmates in their cells. The genius—and horror—of the design was that prisoners would begin to act as if they were always being watched. Even if there was *no one* in the tower, they would regulate their behavior and internalize their own watchguard. By expanding the concept of the panopticon to other systems of power and social control, Foucault demonstrated how modern society was built on such internalized rules and regulations. The eye in the sky in the casino, the traffic cam at the intersection—these all control our behavior by signaling: "You are being watched."

For my mother, growing up under a series of authoritarian regimes and military dictatorships meant continuously being under the gaze of an invisible eye. It knew her name and followed her movements. It relied on a network of informants, who turned in neighbors and family members for the slightest infraction. Even in the United States, where my mother was presumably safe from its surveillance, my mother continued to act as if she were being watched. How many times had she expressed fear when I critiqued systems of power? How many times had she pinched me or physically tried to shut my mouth with her hands? Even her parenting style was authoritarian, modeled on control and fear. I would tell my mother that we weren't living in North Korea, or that the U.S. Constitution protected free speech, but she would scoff at me. "You're so naive," she would say.

The setting may have changed, but in truth, we *were* still under an invisible eye. I'd internalized a whole set of behaviors based on a lifetime of being watched and disciplined by capitalism, racism, and patriarchy. The model minority myth, the white gaze, microaggressions, internalized racism—these were all part of the machinery of control, teaching me how I, an Asian woman living in America, should behave: stay quiet, stay small, work hard, be grateful. Perhaps the methods of social control weren't as obvious as, say, North Korean authoritarianism, but they were just as effective.

I call my mom crazy for believing North Korean spies surveil her, but does that mean I'*m* crazy for believing that white supremacy and its network of informants surveil me today? Anti-Asian discrimination is often coded and implied— "undercover," so to speak. Looking back on what I've written, so many of my experiences with racial discrimination could be dismissed as paranoia.* Maybe my middle school teacher wasn't racist; she just thought my essay was weak. Maybe the lady in the pool wasn't racist; she was just socially inept. Maybe the Atlanta shooter wasn't racist; he was just having a bad day. None of them *said* anything explicitly anti-Asian. I'm the one who is crazy, or "pulling the race card," or falsely claiming victimization.

But how then to explain the body's memory? How to explain the racial sixth sense that so many people of color share? People and systems *are* watching us; they *are* acting against us. Is it no wonder we internalize these beliefs and assume surveillance, even if *no one* is watching?

One of my students, a young Black woman, described driving through a Southern California exurban neighborhood that "felt" racist. Was she being paranoid, or was she picking up on signifiers like American flags and F-150s with NRA bumper stickers? In every academic job I have held, my colleagues of color have warned me of racist administrators and colleagues and structures waiting to sabotage my career. Were they being paranoid, or was this a whisper network to help a junior colleague of color survive a hostile system? Anti-Asian hate crimes have increased exponentially these past few years, so I bought a can of pepper spray. Was I being paranoid, or was I simply trying to protect myself as a small, vulnerable woman of Asian descent?

In 2019, I was getting out of my car and my door clipped the side mirror of a small hatchback speeding past me. The

---

* I want to make clear I'm *not* talking about clinical paranoia, which is a severe and debilitating mental illness. I'm talking about the everyday paranoia/anxiety experienced by people of color in a white supremacist society.

driver screeched to a halt and stormed out of his car in a rage. He was thirty, white, with red eyes. He started screaming profanities at me. We were in the middle of a residential neighborhood at 9:00 A.M., near a fire station and a couple of shops. There were people out walking their dogs and grabbing breakfast at a local café. Yet no one intervened. I was terrified but also enraged. His anger toward me was so entirely out of proportion to what happened. I wanted to scream profanities back at him. I have seen countless acts of road rage, but this was different. This was an act of hate. I could see myself through his eyes—a shitty Asian driver, a foreigner, a piece of shit.

As he was screaming at me (*You FUCKING CUNT, FUCK YOU. What the FUCK were you thinking, YOU BITCH*), I kept thinking, *I wish I weren't small, I wish I weren't Asian, I wish I weren't a woman.* If I weren't so unthreatening, perhaps he'd have thought twice about abusing me in public. Why couldn't I be seven feet tall and ripped? Why couldn't I look like the Rock? I bet if I were a white woman, he wouldn't act this way because I'd remind him of his mom, his sister, his girlfriend.

Instead, I said, "Please don't curse at me."

Weak. I was so weak.

Afterward, I was shaking so hard and thinking so unclearly that I almost drove away with this guy's driver's license. His name was Shawn. I googled him afterward. He'd attended a local Catholic high school, played college baseball, grown up in an affluent neighborhood nearby. He was still on his parents' car insurance. He reminded me of some students at the Catholic university where I now teach. I don't know why I looked him up. Maybe to figure out why he was this way, to try and see the humanity in someone who had dehumanized me? I reminded myself that I had done nothing wrong—that no one deserved to be treated this way. Yet why did I feel like my body had betrayed me? Why did I feel like I had to apologize for my very existence?

This incident happened almost a year before the COVID+ pandemic began. Before Trump's hateful anti-Asian rhetoric and the spike in anti-Asian hate crimes. People could point to this as proof that the man's rage toward me was not racially motivated and that he was therefore an ass-hole, not a racist. But racism doesn't work that way, and the racial imaginary doesn't just turn on and off like a television. The threat of violence and retribution are constant, and incidents like this ensure that I continue to regulate my behavior, *even when no one else is around.*

I no longer leave the house without pepper spray. I avoid walking alone. I've taken to wearing sunglasses, a hat, and a mask when I go outside, all the better to hide my features. Still, every time I see a small gray VW hatchback on the road, I avert my eyes and pray it's not him. Every time I see a fratty-looking white guy in a baseball cap, my chest tightens. I recognize I'm being paranoid. He has probably forgotten all about me. But I know he's out there, and if not him, someone just like him.

Chapter Eleven

IMPOSTOR SYNDROME

[Mental health] is going to be the casualty, the
price they pay for the American Dream.
—Karla Cornejo Villavicencio

Every person of color I know struggles with mental health. Every person of color I know self-medicates in some way, whether it's through drinking or drugs or work or sex. My mom copes with her anxiety/depression/OCD (none of it officially diagnosed) by compulsively exercising, going to church, and shopping at the Salvation Army. I cope with my anxiety/depression (officially diagnosed) by taking Zoloft, drinking too much, and shopping online.

I was almost definitely depressed in high school, but it went unnoticed and untreated. Mental illness was perceived as taboo, a sign of weakness and failure, and the solution was always to suck it up. Did my parents have the luxury of therapy and meds? They didn't even have health insurance, for fuck's sake. My mom's advice was always to pray or take a nap. In college, she would send me Costco-size bottles of Centrum and religious self-help books, which I threw straight into the trash.

Once I left Princeton, I thought my anxiety and depression would lift. I assumed my problem was situational—that once I removed myself from the stressful environment, I would be fine. I failed to realize that the stressful situation was being a woman of color in America, and that there was no escape. I cannot escape my body unless I kill myself. I could move, I suppose, but where to? And would it be any better? Besides, this place is my home. Even if I move, I bring that home with me. To quote Satan in *Paradise Lost*, "Which way I fly is hell; myself am hell."

I secretly wanted to be a writer, but I didn't know how. I had thousands of dollars in college loans to repay. I did not have rich parents who could fund a year of travel to India or cover my tuition for an MFA program or subsidize a magazine internship. Like many immigrant kids, the situation was reversed—I had to take care of my parents now, repaying them for their sacrifices by getting a good job and making a lot of money to take care of them when they could no longer work. As one of my friends jokes, "My parents don't have a retirement fund. *I'm* the retirement fund."

I also lacked evidence that anyone wanted to hear what I had to say. Every day I was being told, implicitly and explicitly, that what I said was unwelcome or wrong. The Korean American novelist Min Jin Lee described taking a creative writing class in college and mostly staying silent until one day, she tentatively suggested that the writer should define Stonehenge for the reader. She recalled her classmates, all white, looking at her with surprise and pity, like, "Who doesn't know what Stonehenge is?" Lee thought of her parents, who worked six days a week at their small, drafty store in Manhattan, who were robbed at gunpoint several times, who did not have the luxury of vacations to England or the luxury of vacations at all. Lee decided to stay in her lane and go to law school.

In my case, I decided to pursue management consulting. The starting salary at my firm was $47,000, plus a $3,000 signing bonus. Today, that would be the equivalent of a starting salary of $85,000, with a $5,500 bonus. I do not make this much money *today*, more than twenty years later. It was like winning the lottery. I was twenty-one years old, and I would be making more money than my parents. I remember a classmate—a white guy—calling me a sellout. He compared me to Judas betraying Jesus Christ "for thirty pieces of silver." (What a tool.) In retrospect, that sanctimony comes from such a place of entitlement and delusion that it makes me laugh. The only people who don't have to worry about money are people who have money.

A couple of months after my graduation trip to Korea, I moved into an apartment in West Hollywood with a roommate, and when I wasn't commuting to the office in downtown LA, I was on a plane to places like Spartanburg, South Carolina, and Houston, Texas, where I sat in windowless conference rooms working on spreadsheets and presentation decks. I lasted six months in that job. I was the only woman in my cohort of eight. The cohort above me also had only one woman, as did the cohort below me—an unspoken quota. I'd joined a huge bro-y fraternity, full of the same casual sexism, classism, and racism I'd witnessed at the eating clubs. The managing director was fond of giving flowery speeches about the company being "like a banyan tree," its roots spreading all over the world, which is a very pretty metaphor until you realize banyan trees are parasitic and eventually strangle their hosts. (He would later get sent to prison for insider trading.)

One of my managers, Brian, a tall white guy with a receding hairline who had graduated from Yale and was famous in the office for being the youngest person to ever become a manager, openly complained about how women had it easier at the firm and were promoted over more qualified men. He and his South Asian buddy, an engineer from a Brahmin family, would jokingly bow to each other, mimicking the "geishas" at the sushi restaurant we ordered dinner from. Our client was an engineering and construction firm in Orange County, which was housed in a sprawling complex in an office park. The engineers all looked like Dwight Schrute, and they hated us, with our Ivy League degrees and cheesy MBA-speak. As the junior-most member of the team, I was given the shit work, like faxing a deck to a partner at 4:00 A.M. when all the lights in the complex shut down—*ka-chunk*—leaving me to pick out the fax number by the glow of the machine's button pad.

I hated the firm's culture: its transparent worship of money, the condescension toward clients, the thin veneer of meritocracy, the long hours and endless travel. I was hired to be a mule, the one who obediently crunched numbers and ordered takeout for the team while blending into the background. It turned out I was pretty lousy at the job. I really hated building spreadsheets. I was chastised for using my expense account to "overtip" taxi drivers and delivery people (my feeble attempt at wealth redistribution). I was yelled at for yawning in front of a partner. (Yawning is a fear response.

I yawned because I was terrified of this partner, and because I pulled an all-nighter to get him a deck, *not* because I thought he was boring. Though he undoubtedly was.)

The one mentor I found was a woman named Lena who had grown up during the final years of the Cultural Revolution and earned a PhD in physics in the United States before moving into consulting. Lena was ferociously smart and self-confident, with a photographic memory for numbers and facts. She was married and was raising two young children; she drove a minivan, wore cheap suits, and eschewed all the flashy trappings of success. I worked with her on a three-person team advising a small biotech company, and I found her to be an inspiring manager and leader. Yet I watched as the junior associate, a white man named Trevor with close-set eyes fresh out of business school who *loved* talking about his time in the military, repeatedly throw tantrums and threaten to quit the team. He complained to Lena's superiors, calling her overly controlling and insufficiently respectful of his (bad) ideas. He disparaged her to me, calling her a weak leader and patronizingly offering to show me how things *should* be done. Watching them spar, I saw his incredulity that this small Asian woman with an accent *would not* back down. She was way tougher and smarter than he was; she was not scared of him.

Lena left a short while later, recruited by another company after recognizing that she would never be promoted to partner. She'd hit the glass ceiling. Not only were there no women in partnership, but there were also no women of Asian descent in *any* senior role. How could she gain the confidence of those above her when even her subordinates questioned her authority? It didn't matter how hard Lena worked or how good she was: she now had a reputation for being an "ineffective" manager, a reputation seeded by this junior associate. The fact that she had been a great manager to *me* did not matter at a firm in which women and people of color were overwhelmingly in the lower ranks. It was up or out. She chose out.

I followed suit and quit a short time later. I had never quit anything before. I'd been taught that "winners never quit; quitters never win" and that success was more about pain endurance than talent. But now I wondered what prize I was chasing. I didn't want to go to business school or become a managing partner; I wanted to step off the treadmill. Still, I knew that if I quit, I'd confirm all of Brian's biases—that women were less capable, that I'd been hired over a more qualified man. I could feel myself getting sucked into the vortex of stereotype threat: the more pressure I put on myself to prove women weren't affirmative action hires, the worse I performed. When Lena and I both quit within the space of two months, I knew Brian and Trevor wouldn't see it as a sign of systemic problems; they'd see it as proof that the meritocracy worked.

I quit anyway. With no other job lined up, I moved back into my childhood home, spending each day in bed. My parents kept telling me to snap out of it, but all I could do was cry. I felt like I had disappointed them, even though they didn't tell me they were disappointed. I felt like a burden, even though they didn't tell me I was a burden. I'd paid down as much of my student loans as I could, and now I was broke. I tried to withdraw money from an ATM only to discover my balance was negative when the machine ate my card. I was lucky to have a place to return to. To my parents' credit, my mental breakdown was sufficiently worrying that they found me a geriatric Jewish psychiatrist who worked out of his home office in Westwood. He prescribed me tranquilizers, which I did not take, and told me to get a new job, which, duh.

During this time, I'd often meet up with my friend Eileen, a fellow burnout. She'd been born in Korea but moved to the States when she was seven. Her parents were divorced—a rarity in those days—and the children had been divvied up. Eileen went with her mother; her younger sister and brother went with her father. For the next ten years, Eileen had zero contact with her siblings and father, effectively becoming an only child. Eileen's mother remarried, and she and Eileen's stepfather ran a liquor store and then a small market. As a teen, Eileen would help out at the liquor store, watching older white girls from our high school stroll in with their fake IDs to buy cigarettes and beer. Each time her parents accepted their IDs, she knew they were risking their liquor license, while the underage girls were risking nothing more than a slap on the wrist. During the LA Uprising, she watched as gas stations and stores went up in flames just blocks from her apartment in Koreatown. Her parents were miles away in Long Beach, trying to lock up their market while customers pleaded to be let in so they could stock up on food and other necessities.

At our high school, where she was on scholarship, Eileen was a standout, a gifted artist, the only Asian girl on the varsity volleyball team, a champion debater, and a member of student council. Returning home from a debate tournament one evening, still giddy with excitement, she could immediately sense that something was wrong. Her mother informed her that they were headed to the hospital because her stepfather had been shot in a robbery. Eileen felt her elation turn into a guilt so crushing that she began to cry. While she'd been enjoying herself at the tournament, her parents had been risking their lives. When Eileen got into Harvard, it was as if everything—the divorce, the family separation, the shootings, the riots—had been worth it. She had made all her mother's sacrifices worthwhile.

The story was supposed to end there, on a note of triumph. A nice, tidy, model minority fairy tale. But mental health is the casualty of the American dream, and it will catch up with you eventually. Halfway through college, Eileen's mother and stepfather divorced. Eileen found herself coming apart, rebelling against her mother in a way she'd never dared to in high school. For the first time, she admitted to her mother that she'd been sexually abused by her stepfather. She stopped going to class. Her grades plunged. She didn't hand in papers and failed a bunch of classes. Placed on academic probation, she was asked (told) to take a year or two off school to get her shit together. When she told her mother she was coming home, her mother's response was, "What will I tell my friends? What will they think?"

Eileen moved back home, into a small duplex on the border of Koreatown where her mother now lived. We took to meeting up regularly to smoke and drink coffee. Eileen was always late—and not just by a few minutes but by a few hours. Sometimes she fell asleep and forgot to set the alarm. Other times she just couldn't muster up the energy to get out of bed. It didn't bother me—punctuality now seemed trivial without the structure of school or work.

I don't remember what Eileen and I talked about. Probably about how we were high-functioning depressives who suddenly became marginally functioning/nonfunctioning burnouts. Occasionally, we were joined by Eileen's sister, Jennifer, whom she'd reconnected with after a separation of more than ten years. Jennifer and her brother had been raised in Gardena by their father and stepmother. Jennifer did not go to Harvard. She didn't go to college at all. She'd ended up rolling with a Korean gang and spent time in juvie. When I met her, she was strung out on meth and making money by working as a hostess at a booking club in Koreatown. Jennifer was supposed to be the "bad" Korean; we were supposed to be the "good" ones. But there was no real difference between us—just different ways of trying to belong, different drugs of choice, and different strategies of survival as Asian women in America. The end result was the same: we were all drunk, unemployed/underemployed, depressed, and eating huevos rancheros at Swingers at four in the morning.

* * *

Over the next few years, I took a series of underpaid jobs that were tangentially related to art and writing. For a year, I taught English at a Jewish day school, where the students called me Lucy Liu. I moved to New York City and got an assistant position for a once-famous writer of color (a descriptor he would *hate*). Foolishly, I'd hoped he'd serve as a mentor, but instead I spent my days flipping through Sotheby's catalog and helping him bid on epergnes and torchères.* (Once, he purchased a $30,000 chest of drawers and asked me to research insurance premiums. Meanwhile, I was making less than $30,000 a year and was uninsured. I quit.) I managed

---

* My boss explained to me that an epergne is a silver centerpiece that can hold something "like a pineapple." A torchère is apparently a fancy antique version of the cheap halogen lamp I had in my dorm room.

to land a government fellowship that covered tuition for an MFA program but was then rejected from every MFA program I applied to. In the end, I applied to doctoral programs in English, which I thought would allow me to write *and* eat. When I was admitted to Harvard and offered a living stipend of $18,000 a year and health insurance, I jumped at the opportunity.

I started antidepressants after my first semester of graduate school. I'd already been warned that "everyone" is depressed in grad school. You're broke and constantly reminded of your own stupidity or inadequacy. It's part of the hazing culture endemic to elite white spaces, and like Princeton, the Harvard English Department was very elite and very white. In my naivete, I'd assumed that a community of people devoted to literature would be kinder and more humane than one devoted to, I don't know, making a shit ton of money. But as I soon found out, academia is no different from other systems of power in this country. It was full of big names and big egos, but it had a poverty of spirit, a culture of intellectual stinting and hoarding.

In *Heavy*, Kiese Laymon describes the "meager" quality of whiteness, which seemed always to discipline Black people (you're too Black, too loud, too poor, too fat). Behind this contempt is fear: the fear of losing the entitlements of whiteness, like security, wealth, social mobility. There is never enough to go around, and thus you must protect and hoard what you have, even if you have *everything*. Laymon contrasts this with what he calls "black abundance"—a generosity of spirit, love, and community that has nothing to do with material wealth. Among his family and friends, he finds a culture of plenitude that tells him he *is* enough, that he is *more than enough*. It is a small pocket of resistance in a world that is constantly telling him the opposite.

White supremacy culture *is* scarcity culture. It relies on gatekeeping, shaming, and exclusion. It occasionally lets some nonwhite people through, but only those who adhere to its codes of behavior and are content with token status (and willing to fight other nonwhite people who threaten that status). It continually reinforces itself through the distribution of everything from jobs and salaries to mortgages, health care, and education. Even in the midst of incredible wealth (Full scholarships with all-you-can-eat buffets! A ticket to Wall Street!), there is never enough. It's a zero-sum game. I learned this lesson in college. I learned this lesson at my consulting job. I would learn it again in graduate school. I am still learning it.

My first semester of coursework, I finally went to the dentist. I didn't have insurance for the previous couple of years, but now I was on student health insurance and immediately made an appointment at the dental clinic. It was too late. A cavity that had gone untreated was so severe that I would need a root canal—and the cost wouldn't be covered by my crappy student insurance. I sat in the atrium of Mount Auburn Campus Center and cried. I needed $2,500 and had no clue where I'd get it (my graduate stipend broke down to $1,300 a month). Meanwhile, my tooth was throbbing and did I also mention that it was finals week and I had three seminar papers due over the next few days?

I heard that one of my English professors, a tall, patrician WASP whose class I was taking, was looking for a research assistant, and I eagerly set up a meeting. We discussed my seminar paper first, and then I told him about my dental predicament and explained I would be grateful for the job. Dr. Tool, as I'll call him, hemmed and hawed and finally said, "Well, I'd really rather have an assistant who was invested in my research project, not someone who was just doing it for the money." I was mortified. I assured him I was intellectually committed and wasn't just looking for a handout, that I didn't mean to offend him. But it was no use. As he walked me out of his office, he said, "Why don't you just have your parents pay for your root canal?"*

Meager.

This is an example of white supremacy culture. Some white people recoil when I use the term, because they think white supremacy means the KKK and the n-word, and they desperately want to distance themselves from *that* kind of "bad" white person. But white supremacy is everywhere in our culture, and we are all bathed in it. As Ijeoma Oluo writes, "Ours is a society where white culture is normalized and universalized, while cultures of color are demonized, exotified, or erased."† Centering whiteness *is* a form of white supremacy.

Some might argue that my exchange with Dr. Tool was classist, not racist. This is a false distinction, because in this country, race and class are inextricably linked. White families have exponentially more wealth than Indigenous, Black, and Hispanic families. Asian Americans, the "model minority," are assumed to be financially well-off, but this, too, is a white supremacist construct. Asian Americans have a higher

---

* He ultimately hired one of my classmates, a white man whose dad had a Harvard MBA and could definitely pay for his son's root canal.

† See Ijeoma Oluo, *Mediocre: The Dangerous Legacy of White Male America*.

poverty rate than white people, are less likely to be insured than white people, and many are immigrants who may not be highly educated. Professor Tool undoubtedly thought of himself as a "good white person," but he was an avatar of white supremacy. He expected me to conform to his image of the "ideal" graduate student, someone who was just like himself—an academic who took jobs not for money but for the intellectual reward, who had parents that subsidized their child's career and health insurance. A student who, according to all the statistics, is most likely to be *white*.

I received similar messages in my other classes. In one of my grad seminars, we were assigned Gilbert and Sullivan's *Mikado*, a nineteenth-century comic operetta that relies on British stereotypes of Asian culture. Characters are called racist nonsense names like "Nanki-Poo" and "Yum-Yum," white actors are dressed in yellowface, and Japanese culture is exoticized and caricatured. I waited for someone to acknowledge the operetta's outrageous orientalism, but no one said anything. Finally, I raised my hand. I was the only Asian person in the class, and while I tried to address the play's stereotypes in a detached, analytical manner, I could tell the professor, a white woman, was irked. She obviously had a great deal of affection for the operetta (I love patter-songs, too!) and thought I was taking it too personally with my racial critique. I was misunderstanding that the operetta was really a critique of *British* culture. I pushed back, saying that I'd been nicknamed "Yum-Yum" by a middle school history teacher and found the name infantilizing and, frankly, dehumanizing and sexualizing. *The Mikado* might seem an innocuous comedy to a white viewer, but to me, it was clearly minstrelsy. Silence. A white student asked to

change the subject. Once again, I was being a "bad" graduate student. I was critiquing the text as an emotional person
of color, not as an "objective" white person.

It's no wonder I felt like an impostor in grad school. I
was being told *every day* that people like me did not belong.
One of my white professors called Public Safety on a Black
student who was doing filing work outside his office because
she was playing hip-hop too loudly. This man had spent his
entire educational life—college, grad school, professional
career—in the Ivy League. Instead of asking the student to
turn down her music, he assumed she didn't belong there
and called security. I was less racially threatening than the
Black student, but he policed me as well—critiquing the
way I spoke (too modest, with a "girlish" uptick), what I
studied (race), and how I responded to advice (with insufficient compliance). I was simultaneously too "Asian" (too
humble, too "small") and not "Asian" enough (disobedient,
interested in race). He wanted me to be a model minority
automaton, an Asian woman in whiteface.

I swear I didn't start grad school feeling like an impostor. I walked in thinking I was a badass. Yet within six
months, I was getting my first script for Zoloft because I
was having a nervous breakdown. People joked that the
mental health center gave out antidepressants like candy
because everyone at Harvard was used to being the best, so
any "failure," however small, was psychologically devastat-
ing. That was part of it, for sure, but this so-called failure
has higher consequences when you have more to lose—
when you're fighting stereotype threat ("You only got in
because you're Black"; "You can't be struggling because
you're Asian"), when you feel incredible pressure to suc-

ceed in these environments because you gotta represent and pave the way.

In 1998, the same year that I graduated from college, a senior at Columbia University named Shirley Yoon committed suicide. Like Elizabeth Shin at MIT, Yoon was a "model" student, yet she was clearly suffering from profound psychic pain. Her death was felt deeply by members of the Asian American community, who recognized in her death a familiar and unspeakable anguish that outsiders could not fully see or understand. Yoon's suicide prompted the professor David L. Eng and psychotherapist Shinhee Han to coin the term "racial melancholia" to describe the collective sadness and guilt faced by Asian Americans as they faced the difficulties of immigration, assimilation, and racialization. Other nonwhite immigrant groups might face similar pressures, but Asian Americans also had to contend with a white supremacist structure that turned them into an army of model minority robots who were prosperous, obedient, hardworking, and didn't cry racial discrimination like "problem minorities." If we failed, it was our fault, not theirs. Our pain was inexpressible because, according to white America, it did not exist. Cathy Park Hong calls this welter of shame, sadness, and paranoia "minor feelings," a "racialized range of emotions" that constitutes the everyday experience of people of color in white spaces.* ·

Whether it's called racial melancholia or minor feelings or impostor syndrome, this pain is one of the unacknowledged symptoms of white supremacist ideology/pathology

---

* See also Anne Anlin Cheng, *The Melancholy of Race: Psychoanalysis, Assimilation, and Hidden Grief.*

in the Asian American community. White supremacy wants us to be quiet about our pain, to pin the blame entirely on our immigrant parents or our own psychological weaknesses. It wants us to think *we're* the impostors when really it's the system that's the sham. That's because we are critical to the pyramid scheme of the American Dream. We are supposed to "solve" the problem of race in America, to prove this place is the land of equal opportunity and absolve white America of blame. No wonder so many of us are cracking under the pressure. We carry our parents' dreams, our community's dreams, and the thousand-pound gorilla that is the white supremacist fantasy of America.

None of the professors I've mentioned would see what they said as racist or white supremacist. They would probably say they were treating me just as they would a white person, that they were "color-blind." But I am not a white person, and I am not a white supremacist version of an Asian person, either. They did not *see* me. They saw a figment of their imagination, just as my eighth grade teacher had seen a figment of her imagination. All of them had betrayed irritation or cluelessness when I did not adhere to the model minority myth—when I said I needed money, when I spoke of racism, when I wasn't compliant. They were annoyed by me, and they couldn't figure out why. It was because I was an impostor. It was because I was not white.

* * *

According to a recent study, Asian Americans are the racial group least likely to reach out for help with mental illness. They are three times less likely than white people to seek mental health treatment, and while they report fewer mental health issues than white people, they are more likely to commit suicide. Among Asian Americans, Korean Americans are the most likely to kill themselves. In fact, they are more likely to commit suicide than any other ethnicity. Many are first-generation immigrants who struggle with the cultural stigma against mental illness, the importance of saving face, and the crushing stressors of immigration. For second-generation Korean Americans, the model minority myth further deters them from seeking treatment. You're not supposed to speak up or admit that you're struggling. You've got it pretty good compared to other people of color. Your parents are counting on you to succeed.*

Even if you manage to get a therapist and find the money to pay for it, who will you end up talking to? According to the American Psychological Association, 85 percent of therapists are white, and most, I would hazard to guess, are culturally incompetent. It's hard to explain why you are feeling bad to someone who blames all your problems on your tiger mom or the pathology of Asian culture. It's hard to explain why you are feeling bad to someone who thinks the problem is you and not the system.

One of the most tragicomic therapy experiences I had was when I was pregnant and off my meds. (I do not recommend this. Stay on your meds.) I belonged to an HMO, and my therapist was a white lady with a bad face-lift and a breathy voice. She recommended that I join group therapy, and I reluctantly said OK. Every Wednesday, I joined a group of ten women and one man at the mental health

* I recently learned that two Asian American students at Princeton committed suicide within days of each other in May 2022. One was Korean American, the other Chinese American. No one seems to want to talk about this.

office complex in Baldwin Hills. Everyone was Black except me. The therapist in charge was a paunchy, middle-aged white man, and he would encourage us to talk through our problems and offer one another support. The one man in our group was there under court-ordered anger management therapy, and he was enraged to be there. The women were mostly older, coping with cancer, chronic pain, and the death of loved ones. They asked why I was there, and I mumbled something about being depressed, unemployed, and pregnant. I felt like an asshole.

We all sat there, listening to this white therapist talk about everything except the elephant in the room—that though we had different reasons for being there, our respective mental health challenges could not be disentangled from our experiences as people of color in a white supremacist society. Telling a Black man that he has an anger problem without addressing the system that makes him angry and pathologizes his anger; telling a Black woman not to be depressed without addressing a system that does not acknowledge her pain and dehumanizes her and her family; telling me, an Asian woman, that my problems are "cultural" and look at how much shittier white America treats Black people—the whole experience felt like an exercise in futility. Our problems could not be fixed with breathing exercises.

I sometimes wonder if han is really a cultural euphemism for untreated, chronic mental illness. A way to turn something culturally taboo (depression, anxiety, PTSD) that emerges from unspeakable trauma (war, colonization, immigration, racism) into something utterable and legible. Maybe the term "mental illness" itself is wrong and ableist because the truth is, how can you *not* be "mentally ill" when our society is so fucked up? I wonder if all of this—mental illness, han, racial melancholia—is a manifestation of internalized shame. Disconnected from our parents, disconnected from Asian culture and American culture, disconnected from other people of color—some of us may experience an alienation so profound that we inevitably retreat into depression, dissociation, or even death.

I read somewhere that han is particularly agonizing because it's a paradoxical mix of love and hate. The Japanese brutally oppressed Korea, subjugated its people, destroyed its history and culture. It would be easy for Koreans simply to hate the Japanese. But han is painful because it also encompasses contradictory feelings of respect or envy or desire. As much as some Koreans despise Japan, they also want Japan's respect; they want acknowledgment and recognition. Even the push for reparations for World War II sex slaves, or "comfort women," comes from a desire for Japan to admit not only its own inhumanity, but also the humanity of its Korean victims.

James Baldwin wrote, "I love America more than any other country in the world, and, exactly for this reason, I insist on the right to criticize her perpetually." It would be easy to simply hate this country for its treatment of Indigenous people, Black people, people of color, immigrants, and many more. It would be easier to let its unspeakable acts be forgotten or internalized by its victims/survivors. It would be easier to walk away. Those of us who speak up do so out of a contradictory and masochistic love for this country. We do so because this country is worthy of critique. We do so because we want the country to see us as fully human.

* * *

Zoloft saved my life. But do you know what else saved my life? My friends and professors in the Department of African American Studies. Located in the same building as the English department—in opposite wings—the Department of African American Studies could not have been more different. Where the English department was overwhelmingly white, hierarchical, and marked by a culture of scarcity, the African American Studies department was overwhelmingly people of color and marked by a culture of greater inclusion and warmth. When I crossed the hall, I suddenly became visible. My difference became something to cultivate and celebrate, not control. There's no doubt that it was still an elite, exclusive space (Harvard is gonna Harvard), but there was a tacit acknowledgment that for so many of us who felt cast out, the department provided a refuge.

My friend Laura, who was getting her doctorate in African American Studies, heard of my dental emergency and passed along that Jamaica Kincaid, a faculty member in the African American Studies department, needed a grader. I'd never met Professor Kincaid before, but I was a huge fan of her writing. Born Elaine Potter Richardson in Antigua in the British West Indies, Kincaid moved to New York when she was seventeen to work as an au pair for a wealthy white family. She was unapologetically different—six feet tall and model thin, with shaved eyebrows, a super-short platinum blond haircut, and a wardrobe of vintage hats and jodhpurs.

She changed her name to Jamaica Kincaid when she became a published writer, and she went on to have a long and esteemed career at the *New Yorker*, where she wrote cutting indictments of colonialism and racism. She was like no professor I'd ever had before—a Black woman, an immigrant, and entirely self-made.

Professor Kincaid knew she had haters, but she Did Not Give a Fuck. To me, she offered a life-saving piece of advice: "You must bite the hand that feeds you." White supremacy culture expected Kincaid to be grateful and compliant for being allowed into privileged spaces—the *New Yorker*, Harvard, the United States. When she dared mount a critique of power, she was accused of being unworthy or unqualified or angry. But Kincaid refused to apologize for her presence; she refused to bite her tongue. I once saw her give a public lecture in which she condemned this country's history of anti-Blackness. An old white man in the crowd raised his hand and yelled, "If you hate this country so much, why don't you go back to where you came from??!" Kincaid looked at him serenely and said, "Why don't *you* crawl back into the hole *you* came from?"

Kincaid hired me as her grader, and as I sat in on her class, I watched as she challenged and often frustrated students who wanted easy answers and easy A's. (Nobody feels as entitled to an A as a Harvard student.) At the end of the semester, Kincaid told me we'd gotten the worst batch of teaching evaluations she'd ever seen. The students hated Kincaid because she did not teach or look like Dr. Tool, and who did she think she was? The students hated me because I did not give them A's, and who did I think *I* was?

"Whatever," Kincaid said. Then she invited me to Seder

at her friend's house. And to her home in Vermont, where I helped her pick asparagus from her garden. And to Death Valley, where we searched for wildflowers. She read at my wedding. She cuddled my babies.

Abundance.

Part III

GRACE

Chapter Twelve

BOTH/AND

Several years ago, my African American literature class was reading Ralph Ellison's *Invisible Man*. First published in 1952 and loosely based on Ellison's own life, the novel follows its unnamed protagonist from a childhood in the Jim Crow South to college at an all-Black institution (modeled on Tuskegee Institute) to his time in Harlem, where he joins and then disavows the Communist Party (the "Brotherhood"). His whole life, the Invisible Man grapples with his invisibility—he's a "spook,"* a spy, a ghost, a stereotype. He's treated like cheap entertainment by white folks, a race traitor by his college president, and a puppet and exotic fetish by his comrades. Everywhere he goes, he faces white systems of power intent on suppressing and erasing him—government, school, factory, hospital, union, political party.

One of my students raised her hand. She was Black and queer, and she asked me with an edge of despair in her voice, "So what do we do now? How can we fight

---

* A "spook" is a ghost, but also a term for a spy and a racial epithet for a Black person.

racism when history is against us? When all the systems are against us?"

I felt my heart lurch into my stomach. I was looking at thirty faces expectantly waiting for my answer. Trump had just been elected, several of my undocumented students had disappeared from class, and a right-wing student group had built a janky wall out of cardboard boxes in the middle of campus.

We're fucked, I wanted to say. And yet I couldn't get the words out of my mouth. I couldn't say those words and watch her face fall as the class collapsed with me into a pit of futility and despair. I thought back to Ellison's epilogue, as the Invisible Man retreats from the world and bides his time underground, siphoning power from the electrical grid, gaining strength, getting ready to reemerge. So I said something that I hoped—and still hope—is true. "You have to fight," I said. "You have to be a spy. You have to infiltrate systems of power, and then you need to challenge them from within."

I've thought of that moment a lot over the last several years as I've found myself teetering again between cautious hope and abject despair when it comes to racism in this country. Anger and cynicism are my default mode, survival tactics honed over years of disappointment. Better to say we're fucked than get your hopes up, only to have them dashed. I'm a pessimist and a hater, a Debbie Downer and a depressive. I always see the glass as half empty. It's how I've managed to get through life.

But I'm also a teacher, which means I'm stupidly idealistic. I can't wallow in despair, because if I do, I'll just lie down and die. I can't wallow in despair, because if I do, I deny people's capacity to change—my students' capacity to change, and my own. I've squirreled my way into systems of power. Now what do I do to challenge those systems?

* * *

The instructor said,

Go home and write
a page tonight.
And let that page come out of you—
Then, it will be true.

I wonder if it's that simple?
            —Langston Hughes, "Theme for English B"

I now teach writing to first-year college students, and I often turn to Langston Hughes's "Theme for English B" on the first day of class. In the poem, the instructor is an older white man; his student is young and the only Black student in the class. The instructor assigns a seemingly straightforward autobiographical prompt; the student mulls over the assignment. A vast gulf separates him from his professor—the gulf of race, class, age, privilege. Can a single page bridge that gulf? Can language span the divide? Is it really so simple?

There will always be a divide between instructor and student, writer and reader. And for a long time, I was not interested in bridging that divide. I was more focused on defending myself and proving myself to real and imagined white interlocuters. As a student, I mostly wrote for white teachers. As a scholar, I mostly wrote for the white academy. As a teacher, I mostly taught white students. I was trained to write and teach defensively, earning respect by comporting myself according to the codes of whiteness.

When I first began teaching high school English in 1999, I was frequently mistaken for a student myself, so I took to wearing suits and pulling my hair back in a bun. I was so strict that the students called me General Lee (the irony of this is not lost on me). My older, white, male colleagues could roll into class wearing a ratty T-shirt and Birkenstocks and have their students call them "Bob," yet still be taken seriously. Me, on the other hand? I needed every last bit of authority I could grasp. I learned, as one of my friends put it, to dress like an old, rich white lady and act like an old, rich white man. I *was* General Lee.

Some of my students still refused to take me seriously. The worst offenders—and this should come as no surprise—were white men. One of my college students, a film production major who took phone calls in class, deflected me when I asked him to put away his device. "Come on, Jules!" he joked. Another student asked me if English was my first language because the way I "moved my mouth" led him to believe I was a non-native speaker. I'd been called the name of every Asian female teacher on campus—by students and by colleagues. Every professor of color has similar stories.

But something changed when my classroom became more "diverse" and "nontraditional." In 2013, I began a job at the University of Nevada, Las Vegas, a large public institution where 67 percent of students identify as an ethnic or racial minority, making it one of the most diverse universities in the country. For the first time, I taught in a classroom where people of color were in the majority. Meanwhile, many of my students had never had a nonwhite professor before. The ground had shifted in the classroom. There was still a gap between us, but it had narrowed.

Without realizing it, I had perfected a teaching persona that was based on my experiences in elite white spaces. I had spent years hiding behind my degrees and my clothes and my CV, using it to project an image of invulnerability. But now I was exhausted. And I realized these students weren't my enemies—they were like me. They were the children of immigrants, they were juggling multiple jobs, they had kids and aging parents. They dealt with everyday acts of racism, they didn't have money for bus fare, they loved reading and wanted to become writers. Most of all, they were curious and eager and idealistic and humble, and they were extending to me a courtesy I could not give myself. They were showing me grace.

I had to relearn how to teach. Instead of centering my white students, I had to center my students of color. I had to unlearn years of white supremacy. I had to unlearn my academic training and the perverted rewards system, which sees teaching as secondary (and worthless) compared to publishing or winning grants. I had to care less about the moments of disrespect—moments that always flooded me with shame—and care more about the moments of communion. It's hard. I am trying.

I see you. I see the student who sits quietly at the edge of the classroom, who feels like college is perhaps not for them or that they don't fit in. You might be invisible to the outside world, but you are not invisible to me. Invisibility, it turns out, is relative. As Toni Morrison points out, the Invisible Man is not invisible to everyone. "Invisible to *whom*?" she asks. "Not to me." Take away the lens of white supremacy and the Invisible Man becomes visible. Flick off "the little white man that sits on your shoulder and checks out everything you do or say," she says. "You sort of knock him off and you're free."

I had to relearn how to write. For most of my life, I've written for an imagined reader who is, by default, white and elitist and old. I learned to wield the language of power, which was purposefully exclusive and obscure, meant to keep people out rather than invite them in. The people who evaluated my journal submissions, my job applications, my book proposals were mostly white. My dissertation, my first published academic book—who was I writing for? Not my parents, who couldn't make heads or tails of the literary jargon I used. Not my students, who were considered by my peers too unsophisticated to understand elite scholarly discourse. I'm not saying this kind of writing is worthless; I am saying that it centers and prioritizes a reader that I am no longer interested in addressing.

My student asked me, "So what do we do now?" She asked, "How can we fight racism when history is against us? When all the systems are against us?"

I am a straight middle-aged Korean American woman. My student was a queer Black woman in her early twenties. A vast gulf separated us—the gulf of race, class, sexuality, age, privilege. The systems of white supremacy, of heteropatriarchy, of capitalism had helped to create that gulf. But my student said "we," and she included not just me but everyone else in that classroom. Racism and systems of oppression affected *all of us*, some more violently and more insidiously than others, but it was up to all of us to recognize our common humanity, band together, and figure out a way to fight back.

* * *

When I began graduate school, I wanted to specialize in nineteenth-century British literature. I had fallen in love with George Eliot's *Middlemarch* and her compassionate moral vision. But during my first year of coursework, at the same time I began working for Jamaica Kincaid, I decided to take a class with Henry Louis Gates, Jr., the literary scholar and public intellectual. I initially hesitated to enroll because I thought it wasn't meant for me—someone who wasn't Black and who knew very little about Black literature. I took the class because Professor Gates had been nice to my parents once. He won't remember this, but in my first week of grad school, my parents—who, like many Korean immigrants, worshipped at the altar of Harvard—came to visit me in Cambridge. I took them to Barker Center, where the English department and African American Studies department were located. As we walked up to the building, we passed Professor Gates. He was elegantly dressed, walking down the ramp with his cane. I felt myself getting flustered. He had no idea who I was, but I obviously knew who he was. I'd seen him on TV.

As we passed each other, he smiled and said hello. I almost fell down. And then he turned to my parents and greeted them as well. My parents had no idea who he was, but they smiled back shyly and said hello. It was a small thing, but if you are a person of color in a predominantly white space, you get used to being invisible. Professor

Gates saw me, and more importantly, he saw my parents. I will always remember that.

I ended up working with Gates on a dissertation examining the intersections between African American and British literature. When I graduated in 2008, I tried to get a job as a Victorianist because I didn't think I could, or should, get a job as an African Americanist. But whether it was because of the terrible economy or the overwhelming whiteness of academia, I failed. I encountered meagerness at every turn. There were no jobs. My research was questioned, my publications dismissed, my accomplishments attributed to nepotism or favoritism or lowered standards. At one interview at an Ivy League university, a famous white literary theorist picked me up in his son's car, complaining about the rap music his son listened to. "It's all 'n—r, n—r, n—r,'" he said, laughing. I didn't say anything. I bit my tongue. I really needed the job. (I did not get the job.)

People told me I should have specialized in Asian American literature because then, at least, I'd be "marketable." A white senior scholar, hearing about my research, warned me not to tread on his turf. Another assumed my parents were professors because how else would I have gotten here? I was told to stop being so modest, to be more assertive and self-promoting. At the same time, I was told to stop publishing so much because I came across as arrogant and intimidating. A white faculty "mentor" advised me to hide in my office and avoid talking to anyone so I wouldn't rub anyone the wrong way. The people who gave me this advice were all white. They were indoctrinating me into the white supremacist logic of academia, putting me in my place and defending white mediocrity. Some were trying to help me. Some were trying to sabotage me. But I was not white, and all these jobs, save one, went to white candidates.* I fell into a deep depression, I got pregnant, I decided to leave academia.

Unexpectedly, I was invited to apply for a job teaching African American literature at UNLV. Only afterward did I learn that Professor Gates had recommended me for the position. It was a "target of opportunity" hire, meaning I was a member of an underrepresented group, which in 2013 included Asians Americans.† Professor Gates made it clear to the search committee that I was not Black—that I was *Korean American*—but that I had been thoroughly trained and he could vouch for my scholarship and teaching. I submitted my application and forgot about it. I had a two-year-old daughter and was now pregnant with my second child, which, as everyone knows, makes a person a super attractive job candidate. I was stunned—incredulous, really—when I got the job.

And then I freaked out. I was grateful to be employed, of course. But I wondered if I had the right to teach Black literature when I didn't have the lived experience of being Black. I wondered if I got the job because the department was so hostile to Black people that I was an "acceptable" compromise (the model minority!). I wondered if I was the undeserving beneficiary of Harvard's old-boy network, even though I was not white and I was not a boy. I worried

---

* One job went to a Latino candidate. He was denied tenure and left academia.
† Asian Americans were dropped from this category a few years later, after our faculty numbers across the university reached about 15 percent, the proportion of Asian Americans in the student population. Meanwhile, the English department remains 85 percent white on a campus where BIPOC students make up 65 percent of the population. The department currently has *zero* professors of Asian descent.

my colleagues would dismiss me as an affirmative action hire. A Chicano colleague warned that students might be leery of me, viewing me as an interloper or impostor. *I* felt like an interloper and impostor.

In the end, all of these things were true and none of them were true. I was a "diversity" hire who was later told by a white colleague that I didn't actually count as diverse. I had students who looked at me askance when I walked into the classroom and many more who welcomed my perspective. Everyone thought I was an ally. No one thought I was an ally. Everyone thought I was an enemy. No one thought I was an enemy. I was not white, I was not Black. I was neither/nor.

It's a crazy-making existence. In the words of actor Steven Yeun, "The Asian American experience is what it's like when you're thinking about everyone else, but nobody else is thinking about you." Asian Americans operate from a position of existential invisibility. You're not one thing or another, you're a cipher, you're whatever people want to project onto you. As Charles Yu writes in *Interior Chinatown*, you are literally the "third person," the "extra," the Generic Asian Man in the buddy cop show called "Black and White." Nobody notices when you're there, and nobody notices when you're gone.

However, the Invisible Man recognizes that invisibility can be a superpower. He's a shape-shifter and a ghost, impossible to pin down. "Change the joke and slip the yoke," Ralph Ellison once wrote to a friend. White supremacy can't see you. White supremacy has blinders on that imagines you as weak, silent, forgettable. For Asian Americans, that's a condition of incredible erasure, but maybe, maybe, it's also a position of potential power. As Cathy

Park Hong notes, invisibility can be "weaponized." We can change the joke, slip the yoke, and wield our invisibility to sabotage white supremacy. And you know what? *They won't even see us coming.*

Invisible to whom? I am not invisible to my Asian American compatriots. I am not invisible to my fellow people of color and Indigenous allies. I am not invisible to my students. Nor are they invisible to me. There is a huge community of us out there. My allegiance is to them. We have to break out of the clusterfuck that is race in this country and stop being used as a pawn and scapegoat of white supremacy. I am the third person, the extra, the bystander. But I am also *the* third person, the narrator, the witness. I am inside the story and outside the story. I am everywhere and nowhere, and I want to fuck things up.

* * *

In August 2020, I took an antiracism workshop moderated by a diversity coach and open to members of my high school class. I'm generally leery of diversity workshops, seeing them as about as effective as sexual harassment trainings, meaning: not effective at all. My friend had organized the event, and I told myself I was there to support her. Most of the participants were white, and many were women I had reviled as a teenager. Now they wanted to "become allies" (I had to stop my eyes from rolling right out of my head). I was one of a handful of nonwhite participants, and I sat back, feeling contemptuous and superior. My former classmates were clamoring for checklists and reading lists. Should I donate to this organization or that one? Is this the right or wrong way to be an ally? It was like they wanted to finish the workshop, get an antiracism badge, and be absolved of their racial sins.

The moderator, a Black woman, cautioned all of us against assuming antiracist work was ever done. And then she said something that shook my entire way of thinking. She said each of us need to move away from thinking in binaries. Right versus wrong, good versus evil, even racist versus antiracist— these are all too simplistic. They don't capture the messiness of humanity or the fact that we are always suspended between two poles. Sometimes we're right, sometimes we're wrong. Sometimes we're good, sometimes we're bad. Sometimes we're racist, and sometimes we're antiracist. "Instead of thinking in terms of either/or, think in terms of both/and," she said.

I turned off my Zoom video and started weeping uncontrollably. Because even though what the moderator was saying was basically what I tell my students ("literature is about ambiguity") and how I'd been trained ("deconstruction is the critique of binaristic oppositions"), I hadn't realized that I'd fallen into the same trap. I'd spent my entire life caught in a racial binary that canceled me out. Now, I was being asked to look at myself in a different way, to see myself as a both/and instead of as a neither/nor. I was both white adjacent and racially othered; a person of color and someone excluded from that category; racially privileged and also disadvantaged.

What this also meant is that I had an ability—a curse, but also a gift—to slip into different spaces. I know what it's like to survive in predominantly white spaces. I know what it's like to find safety and solidarity in nonwhite spaces. I know what it's like to be a student in a classroom and be the butt of a racist joke. I know what it's like to be a teacher in a classroom and to explain why the joke is racist. I am an insider and an outsider, a spy and an ally. I am both/and.

The truth is, a lot of us don't fit into easy binaries, whether we're Asian American or Latinx or Indigenous or multiracial or queer or gender nonbinary or none of these things or all of these things. Categories are slippery, and no one understands this better than young people. Old people like to trash young people—I have been guilty of this myself—but the young people I have met are more empathetic, tolerant, compassionate, and flexible than those of us who are older and jaded. And they're already infiltrating and challenging systems of power—in their families, in their schools, in their workplaces.

But they—we—can't do it alone. For those of us who are in a position of privilege, especially Asian Americans who have benefited from white supremacy and white adjacency, this is an opportunity and obligation to do more. To advocate, to resist, to speak up, and not just on behalf of the most vulnerable members in the Asian American community, but on behalf of other vulnerable communities of color, too. I'm talking to you, fellow Gen Xers and millennials, stuck between the Boomers and the Zoomers. I'm talking to you, fellow 1.5- and 2nd-generation immigrant kids, who have always served as the conduit among cultures, languages, generations, races. Some of us have platforms. Some of us have power. Let's use it on behalf of those who don't.

This means rejecting anti-Black racism within our own families and communities, as well as in the predominantly white communities of power that we have infiltrated. When an Asian person says anti-Black shit to me, they assume I am on the side of anti-Blackness and white adjacency. Fuck that. I am not that kind of Asian. When a white person says anti-Black shit to me, they assume I am on the side of anti-Blackness and white supremacy. Fuck that. I am not their Oriental. I'm a double agent and I am a traitor. These people don't see me. But I can see them.

* * *

Recently, a Vietnamese American student in my African American literature class visited me during office hours. She was from a predominantly white community in the Midwest, and she rarely spoke in class. I encouraged her to participate more, but she expressed serious misgivings.

"What are you worried about?" I asked.

"Well, you know how Black people are really sensitive about race?" she said, lowering her voice. "My mom told me that if I accidentally say the wrong thing, they'll beat the shit out of me."

I was stunned. It was halfway through the semester, and I had clearly done a really crappy job if this student was still subscribing to stereotypes that we'd spent weeks dismantling. I could hear my mother's voice in this student's mother's voice—the voice of an immigrant who wanted her daughter to stay out of trouble, to keep her mouth shut, to see Black people as a problem minority and to ally herself with white supremacist beliefs. She was being an obedient daughter, and she was telling me this because I was Asian and she assumed that I would understand.

And I did understand, sort of. But I also knew that her mother was wrong, that these were anti-Black stereotypes calculated to drive a wedge between her and other people of color, that the people most likely to kick the shit out of her were white supremacists convinced she was stealing their jobs or working for a foreign government. Staying silent about racism would not protect her, just as avoiding controversy would not protect her. As I tried explaining this to her, I knew I was asking her to do more than unlearn her racist assumptions. I was asking her to betray her mother and reject what she'd been taught in the way I'd rejected what I'd been taught. I was asking her to change the way she saw herself.

I thought about this student when COVID+ shut down campus the following semester and she had to fly home to Minnesota. In the early days of quarantine, my Asian American students had immediately noticed a spike in anti-Asian hostility. A Filipina student in my first-year seminar wrote about going to a Target in Orange County and being treated like a pariah by another shopper (*"You're* the reason why people are getting COVID," the customer said). A Vietnamese student swore people were giving her "weird looks" at the grocery store, but she tried to convince herself she was just being paranoid. I knew what she meant. I'd been walking around a nearby park when I saw a white woman heading toward me from the opposite direction. I swear I saw *fear* in her eyes, and she cut a wide berth when she passed by. Was she just practicing appropriate social distancing, or was she worried *I* was "the reason why people are getting COVID"?

I thought about this student again on May 25, 2020, when George Floyd was murdered by the police in her hometown of Minneapolis. The white officer who killed Floyd was married to a woman of Hmong descent (she would soon divorce him and publicly disavow his actions). One of the officers who stood by as Floyd was murdered was also Hmong

American.* Throughout the weeks that followed, Black Lives Matter protests were held around the country. In Los Angeles, stores were broken into and looted by opportunists; windows were boarded up; the National Guard showed up in tanks. Sitting at home, I felt agony. It had been nearly thirty years since the LA Uprising, and what I experienced in the collective consciousness and in my own soul was a caustic mix of rememory, han, and PTSD. Another Black person murdered in an act of police brutality captured on video. Another flood of anger and despair and sorrow.

My parents no longer owned a liquor store or a fast-food restaurant, but I felt a tightening in my chest for the immigrant business owners who worried that their livelihoods would be destroyed, and I felt a familiar nausea when white people spoke of BLM protestors as terrorists or thugs. Once again, Beverly Hills fortified its borders. After months of sheltering in place, dutifully obeying city restrictions, I decided to screw it and drove to West Hollywood to join a protest. The pandemic had emptied the streets of their usual traffic, but now it felt like a new occupying force was in town. I passed a tank parked incongruously in front of the Beverly Connection and saw dozens of police officers and National Guard troops milling along a heavily barricaded stretch of Santa Monica Boulevard. *This cannot be happening*, I told myself.

A week later, I attended a protest in Culver City with a couple of friends, and I was heartened to see a large number of Asian American protestors, most under the age of thirty, in the racially mixed crowd. I was struck by the absence of

---

* In July 2022, Tou Thao was sentenced to serve forty-two months in prison for his role in the fatal arrest of George Floyd.

police officers. The march was full of children and music and solidarity, and aside from a brief moment when a white guy stepped onto his balcony to call us Antifa scum, the atmosphere was generally hopeful. I let myself embrace optimism. Here in LA, things were changing, I told myself. We're moving toward cross-racial solidarity. We're rejecting the old racist tropes that pit Black and Asian people against each other.

Across town, on the same day, my former student Tyler was also at a BLM protest. She and her fiancé were marching through Old Town Pasadena when they noticed a white pickup truck covered in right-wing extremist flags gunning its motor and spewing black exhaust over the crowd. The truck drove straight into the crowd, scattering the protestors. In the chaos, Tyler fell and severely bruised her leg. She sent me a photo, telling me how shaken she was after coming close to being killed. She was a Black woman with her Black fiancé marching for Black lives, and some crazy white supremacist had tried to kill them.

Later, the man in the truck was arrested. The white supremacist was a twenty-eight-year-old Chinese American man. In a published photo, he posed in a Three Percenters muscle T-shirt, flexing a bicep. His truck was loaded with illegal firearms, ammunition, an eighteen-inch machete, a metal pipe, and a megaphone. For months, he'd been hoarding weapons and tactical equipment at his family's vineyard in Lodi and at his home in San Marino. Luckily, no one was killed.

Asian Americans are the beneficiaries and the victims of white supremacy, among its most ardent defenders and its most vocal critics. We are stuck in the middle, all of us, but we have a choice. We can uphold the power structure or we can dismantle it. What will we choose to do?

Chapter Thirteen

BITING THE HAND

There was once a Frog Mother who had a very disobedient son. He always did the exact opposite of what he was told. When his mother told him to go up, he went down; when she told him to go right, he went left; when she told him to study, he would play. Frog Mother loved her son, but she despaired at his rebelliousness. "I won't be here forever," she told her son. "Please, please, be a good frog and listen to me." But Frog Son laughed and hopped away.

One day, Frog Mother became very ill. Knowing she was about to die, she called her son to her side. "Please bury me by the riverbank when I pass away," she asked, assuming he'd do the opposite and bury her in the mountain. "I promise," Frog Son said. But when Frog Mother died, Frog Son was overcome with grief and remorse. For once, he decided to do what his mother had asked. So he buried her body by the riverbank, and the next time it rained, her grave was washed away . . . and this is why frogs cry when it rains. (Or, really, this is why Korean kids feel constant guilt about being shitty to their parents.)

Whenever I misbehaved, my mother would retell this

folktale, scaring me so thoroughly that I swore to never pass this story on to my own children. In my mind, even the most trivial act of disobedience put me on the slippery slope to eventually killing her with disappointment and desecrating her body. There are plenty of stories like this in East Asian cultures, all meant to emphasize the importance of filial piety—reverence for one's parents, elders, and ancestors, and the responsibility to honor their sacrifices.

I'm an extremely shitty daughter. Yes, I have fancy degrees and a good job, so my parents must be proud of me, et cetera, but I am cognizant of all the ways I have failed or, in some cases, actively betrayed my parents. Writing this book is only the latest example. I was taught to keep our family secrets tight, and now I'm selling out my family in the most public of ways—through *publication*—and inviting judgment from others. I have done exactly the opposite of what my mother has instructed since I was child: keep my mouth shut and my head down.

Compounding this is the extra special burden that accompanies being the child of immigrants. Karla Cornejo Villavicencio says it best when describing the unspoken contract between immigrant parents and their children: "They give us a better life, and we spend the rest of that life figuring out how much of our flesh will pay off the debt." I will be in debt to my parents for the rest of my life. I will be in debt to them even after they die. There is no amount of success, money, or status that will cancel it out because the debt is incalculable. I could *never* do what my parents did, moving to a foreign country without a job or legal documentation or language skills or family. I could never do that, not even for my own kids, because I am scared and spoiled. I'm American.

Every year, an Asian American student (and/or the child of immigrants and/or a first-gen college student) will enter my office and admit she wants to be a writer or an artist or some other creative profession that fills her with joy but elicits horror in her parents. Even the choice of major—fine arts over premed, English over engineering—becomes an act of betrayal. We are acutely aware of the sacrifices our parents made to send us to school and secure a stable, financially comfortable job. Announcing "I want to be a poet!" or "I want to be an actor!" is like saying, "I want to kill you and throw your body into a river." What do I say to these students? Do what you want and risk killing your parents? Or do what your parents say and risk killing yourself?

* * *

When I was in high school, my sister and I got into a fight over dinner one night. We were eating ramen and I got mad for some reason, flinging my fork on the table before storming off (yes, I ate my ramen with a fork. I am a bad Korean). The fork bounced off the table and caught my sister above her eye, slicing her forehead open. My mom screamed as she frantically tried to staunch the bleeding with paper towels. She rushed my sister to the emergency room and was gone for hours. Though I didn't believe in God anymore, I knelt at our couch and prayed that my sister would be OK.

When they finally came home, my sister's forehead was stitched up and bandaged in gauze and my mother looked exhausted. "The doctor didn't believe me when I told him what happened," my mother said. "He thought I was lying. He thought *I* was the one who hurt your sister." I felt sick to my stomach. What if the doctor called a social worker because he suspected my mother of child abuse, and we were sent to foster care? I'd endangered my whole family by being stupid and hurling a fork.

The next day, my sister lied to our teachers about how she'd gotten the wound. So did I. We feared their judgment; we knew they wouldn't understand. The stitches eventually came out, leaving a shiny scar. My mom sighed whenever she looked at it. She had always rhapsodized over my sister's beautiful forehead (which I mocked as a "fivehead"), and now she saw it as irreparably disfigured.

For years, I harbored immense shame about this incident. Just one inch lower and I could have stabbed her in the eye and blinded her. What a horrible sister and daughter I'd been. Yet I'd also grown up in a house full of "chronic angers" and mundane acts of violence, of domestic strife and blind rage.* How many times had my mother thrown things at me? Eileen's mom had once hurled a piece of frozen meat at her face, giving her a black eye that lingered for weeks. Among my Korean friends, we would joke about our parents' preferred tools and methods of corporal punishment—the golf clubs and switches, the hands raised above the head. I was merely replicating the violence I saw around me.

I knew my mother loved me, but it was a brutal, punishing kind of love. It could not be encapsulated in trivial things like words, material gifts, or physical affection. Her love was sublime, practically biblical in its level of suffering and sacrifice. She demonstrated her affection through acts of service, some small (like bringing me a bowl of cut fruit

---

* Robert Hayden's "Those Winter Sundays" is my favorite poem for the way it captures parental love haunted by violence.

when I was studying) and some impossibly large (immigrating). Her love was biblical in another way, too—it was overpowering and oppressive. The level of sacrifice was so extreme that it soon developed its own coercive power. If I rebelled, I would be rebuked, and harshly. I feared disappointing her, but I also feared inciting her physical wrath.

But what if punishing your child is the best—or only—way to love your child? Kiese Laymon describes how his mother pushed him to be perfect; she beat him when he was not. She believed this would shield her Black son from the ravages of white supremacy, but in the end, her love took on the warped contours of racial trauma. "She was whipping me because what I would face from police or white people would be even harsher," Laymon writes. At one point, she pulled a gun on him. Laymon says, "I don't think it was the right thing to do, but I understand why she did it at that point in her life." His mother was terrified of losing her son. She loved him so much she almost killed him.

"I'm not a monster. I'm a mother." That's what the poet Ocean Vuong's mother, a Vietnamese refugee, tells him. She hits him in the face with a box of LEGOs, she draws blood, she apologizes, and she buys him McDonald's. Her love is a re-creation of her own trauma—the trauma of war, violence, displacement. Vuong wonders, "Perhaps to lay hands on your child is to prepare him for war." To lay hands on your child is to beat your child; to lay hands on your child is to bless your child. Vuong's mother works at a nail salon, washing the feet of one white woman after another. Her life is an act of service and an act of survival. She is a monster, *and* she is a mother.

My mother was preparing me for war in the way she herself had not felt prepared, both as a girl during the Korean War and as an immigrant woman in America. She knew that because I was small and Asian and a woman, I could easily be exploited and abused. If her love took on the contours of patriarchy and white supremacy, if her love was violent or brutal, so was the world in which she was trying to help me survive. I am not making an excuse for child abuse and violence; it is life shattering, and it is wrong. Still, I understand how abuse and violence can turn into grotesque proxies for love.

For the children who are the recipients of this punishing kind of love, trauma distorts our relationship to our parents in the same way it distorts our parents' relationship to us. We, too, feel monstrous, trapped in a cycle of intergenerational trauma. We want to love our parents, pay homage to their sacrifices, but how do we do that when suffering and sacrifice are the only ways to demonstrate that love? How do we love our own children when a broken, traumatized love is the only love we have to give?

As a young person, I vowed that I'd never have children. I'd been a terrible child, and I knew I would make a terrible mother. They fuck you up, your mom and dad. The only way to end generational trauma was to follow Philip Larkin's advice: get out as early as you can and don't have kids yourself.*

* * *

Obviously, I changed my mind. I married someone who offered the possibility that maybe I wasn't doomed to repeat

---

* Philip Larkin, "This Be The Verse."

the past. In a moment of reckless optimism, we decided to start a family. I got pregnant quickly and almost immediately thought, *SHIT, what have I done?* For the next nine months, I felt like I was going through the hormonal apocalypse. No pregnancy bliss for me—just anxiety, depression, and gestational diabetes.

My daughter was born in September 2009. After I gave birth, the depression didn't lift. I'd quit group therapy and was still off my meds because I was trying to breastfeed. On top of that, my hormones were going berserk and I was delirious from lack of sleep. Like a lot of mothers, I had trouble breastfeeding. I went to a lactation consultant, an old white hippie who told me I had to "surrender to motherhood" and chastised me for not trying hard enough. Primed to think of motherhood as martyrdom, I listened to her garbage advice until my nipples were so bloody that my breast milk turned the color of Pepto-Bismol and I got mastitis and passed out while walking across the room.

Throughout my first pregnancy and the postpartum months, I kept wondering, *How did my mother do this?* My mother had carried and birthed me in a foreign country, with no family around, while working full-time as a nurse (standing on her feet for hours; moving patients twice her size while fending off racist comments) and fretting constantly that her husband might be killed during a robbery. *How did my grandmother do this?* My father's mother had *eight children*, one of whom died in infancy. She was a refugee, with zero access to medical care or enough food to feed herself and her children. My father remembered coming home from school and discovering that his mother had given birth to another baby while he was gone. There was no midwife, no nurse or doctor, no *lactation consultant*—she pulled the baby out of her own vagina, delivered her own placenta, cut the umbilical cord, bound herself up, and kept going.

I had access to health care, stable housing, food, formula, diapers, family support, and a husband who drove me to doctor's appointments. I'd had a baby shower where friends gifted me Boppies and onesies. Still, I was a wreck. How could this suck even harder than I thought it would? Every time my husband left for work, I felt a combination of despair that he was abandoning me, jealousy that he got to escape, and rage that he did not have lactating breasts. My friends Riva and Chris, both children of immigrants, gave birth around the same time, and we would commiserate over how depleted and alone we felt. Yet none of us felt we had a right to complain. We had to suck it up. Our parents and grandparents had survived so much worse.

As my children grew older, I began to see maternal suffering as a badge of honor, a way to pay homage to my ancestors by continuing their legacy of self-denial and sacrifice. If motherhood didn't hurt, I wasn't doing it right. Yes, my life was bougie compared to my mother's life and my grandmother's life, but I was still out there hustling, pushing myself to try harder and do better for my kids. My greatest gift to my children was to love them the way I'd been loved—with unsentimental toughness. I would pass on to them ancestral values like respect for their elders, modesty, and resilience. *My* kids weren't going to be spoiled or entitled.

Remember how I vowed never to tell my children the story of Frog Mom and Frog Son? Yeah, well, it turns out my kids *never listen to me*. "You'll be sorry when I'm dead!"

I'd screech at them when they were being bratty or selfish. I threatened to break their iPads in half or take a baseball bat to the Xbox. They were getting too comfortable, too coddled. The world was hard, and I wanted them to be prepared. I repeated the same things my mother had said to me: their faces were Asian, the world would see them as foreign and inferior. They would have to work twice as hard and be twice as good in order to get half as far. And even though they were far more privileged than I had been (and I was far more privileged than many people I knew), they could not bask in innocence. I refused to send them out into the world naive and unarmed.

I worried especially about my daughter, who is a much kinder, nicer person than I am. Since babyhood, she has been highly anxious, chewing holes in her clothing, avoiding the spotlight, fearful of social conflict or "drama." She is also profoundly empathetic, with a capacity to feel others' pain so keenly that for a long time, she avoided watching movies because even the *sight* of someone suffering was intolerable. Anxiety and empathy—two sides of the same coin. She is sensitive to the world's discomfort and fear and sadness because she has felt those emotions within herself.

I blamed my mother, the undiagnosed queen of generalized anxiety disorder, for my daughter's genetic legacy. Hypervigilance is encoded in our DNA; it kept my ancestors alive through colonialism, war, and famine. My mother bathed me in stress hormones when I was in the womb, and I passed those genes onto my daughter. *What a crappy inheritance*, I would think to myself. Other people got money or picture albums or jewelry; I got the collective trauma of my ancestors.

"You gotta toughen up," I would warn my daughter.

When she fretted over a playground bully, I would tell her, "You come from a long line of tough Korean women. Halmi would kick that bully's ass." When she panicked over a math test, I'd remind her, "Halmi survived war. You can survive fractions." If my daughter was going to take after my mother, I wanted her to inherit my mother's superhuman willpower as well as her anxiety. My mother had learned to harden herself against the world; I hoped my daughter would as well.

* * *

In late 2019, I went to see the comedian Ali Wong perform at the Wiltern in Los Angeles. Wong had been pregnant while performing her two Netflix comedy specials (respect), and in homage, my friend Riva and I dressed up as her in matching leopard-print outfits and red cat-eye glasses, sticking balloons underneath our dresses so we looked massively pregnant. During her routine, Wong mocked Facebook's Sheryl Sandberg of "lean in" fame. "I don't wanna lean in," she joked. "I wanna lie down." She also shared her mantra about motherhood, distilling it to one sentence: "I have suffered enough." She was over the white feminist industrial complex, the culture of mommy-shaming and the bootstraps mentality that told women if they were failing, they just needed to try harder and suffer more.

Coming out of Ali Wong's mouth, these words were a revelation for me. Frankly, I couldn't believe that someone who looked like me was allowed to say that. I'd spent my life leaning in and suffering. So had my mom. Yet Sheryl Sandberg's slick brand of corporate feminism had framed leaning in as an individual *choice* or attitude adjustment, without considering how race and class and other systems of oppression make "leaning in" another version of being exploited. Now here was Ali Wong saying *Fuck That*. She was not going to apologize for being small, for being Asian, for being a woman, for being pregnant, for being a mother, for being tired, for being crass, for being sick of suffering. She was not going to apologize for being human.

Six months later, the world shut down. We entered a period of crisis—a health crisis, an economic crisis, a racial crisis, a climate crisis, an education crisis, a mental health crisis. My children were lucky; they were shielded from so much of the worst (I thought). But my daughter, who turned eleven early in the pandemic, became more anxious and depressed, unmoored from the communities that kept her grounded—her friends, her teachers, her grandparents. Who could blame her? The world was a garbage fire. Everyone I knew was anxious and depressed. My daughter apologized constantly. She hid from the camera during Zoom class. She confided in her pediatrician that she wanted to kill herself.

I lost it. *Not today, Satan.* I'd prepped her for the everyday racism and sexism she'd face, yet I could never have anticipated the confluence of a global pandemic, a rise in nativism and white supremacist violence, and the breakdown of social structures. Under this unprecedented assault, was it any surprise that she felt the need to apologize for her existence, to make herself invisible? Telling her to suck it up or tough it out now seemed like appallingly bad advice. I was asking her to accept the unacceptable, tolerate the intolerable. How had I unwittingly taught her to internalize and compartmentalize—to see her anxiety as a genetic flaw, her face as an apology, and her empathy as a weakness?

How had I unwittingly done the work of white supremacy on my very own children? *Me*, who had always vowed I would *never* allow my children to be brainwashed the way I had been brainwashed?

I realized that my daughter was simply modeling the ways I treated myself. She was absorbing the unconscious ways I apologized for my presence and held myself to unrealistic standards. I could not allow myself to be human. I could not forgive myself. If I was not perfect and extraordinary, I was a failure, an idiot, a loser. I labeled it tough love and holding myself accountable, but really, I had just internalized what the outside world has told me I must do to be treated as a human. In the process, I became what Layla Saad has described as "an agent of white supremacy against myself." When I made a mistake, as I inevitably did because I am *human*, I punished myself. No one hated me more than me.

Most days, I think I'm a piece of shit. I'd developed an inferiority complex that comes from being an Asian American woman and mother in a society that is constantly telling people like me that we're deficient. To survive, I developed a grinding work ethic, hypercompetency, a capacity to withstand pain. These qualities have undeniably helped me succeed in a white supremacist and capitalist system that depends on the exploitation and obedience of people like me. They've shored up my sense of self-worth and pushed me to excel. But what began as a way to survive in the short-term ends up sabotaging survival in the long-term. The system doesn't care if I break down; the system will just discard and replace me. There has to be a more sustainable way to survive and to succeed that doesn't end in burnout, self-harm, or suicide.

It has taken seeing my friends, students, and own children go through this same logic of self-recrimination and self-hate to realize, *enough*. We are all doing the best we can in a system that has taught us to hate ourselves and punish ourselves. We must allow ourselves to be human, to make mistakes. For far too long, I fetishized suffering—the suffering of my forebears, of han, of immigrant life. I told myself that suffering was central to Korean American identity, that it was my heritage and my superpower. I'm not alone in this. This is something I share with so many other women of color and colonized peoples. We carry survivor's guilt; we remember the struggles of our parents and think, *Shut up and suck it up*. Rocío Rosales Meza, a Xicana/Mexicana healer whose parents and grandparents grew up in poverty, describes her own internal script: "I have to work even harder because my mom and abuelita suffered so much" and "How dare I complain and attend to myself when they had it so much worse?" We think back to ancestors who were colonized or enslaved or displaced or murdered, and we tell ourselves, I *owe it to them* to suffer and to survive.

Well, guess what? We have suffered enough. We have been punished enough. There is no glory in continued victimization and pain. I don't want my students or children to go through what I went through. I do not want them to punish themselves, to haze themselves, to hate themselves. There's a difference between giving them the tools to navigate the world—a decent work ethic, resilience—and turning those tools into cudgels of continued oppression. This is why I so emphatically reject the notion of "paying your dues," especially when it's really code for tolerating abuse. My children should not accept the unacceptable. They should not internalize that they are pieces of shit. They should feel entitled to humanity, to value themselves and each other. I am their ancestor, and I do not want them to suffer. I want them to heal.

In the past several years, the phrase "self-care" has become ubiquitous. I cringed when I first heard it used. It sounded like goop bullshit—the kind of thing rich white women in LA say when getting a mani-pedi or going on a wellness retreat. In my mind, self-care was a euphemism for personal indulgence and vanity. How dare these people act like they *deserved* to take care of themselves? They already had privileged lives. This was just another grotesque act of entitlement.

But when my students used the term, I realized that self-care could be a revolutionary act. As Audre Lorde wrote, "Caring for myself is not self-indulgence, it is self-preservation, and that is an act of political warfare." A student of mine, a young Black woman, pointed out that her level of self-care (getting enough sleep, showering, exercising) was directly correlated to how much she valued herself on any given day. If she thought she was a piece of shit, she treated herself like a piece of shit. If she thought she was precious and worthy, she treated herself as precious and worthy. To treat yourself as human in a world that dehumanizes you—now *that* is an act of resistance.

I laugh when people fret about how young people today don't have grit. They're talking to the wrong young people. Sure, there are bratty young adults, just like there are bratty old adults—I work with some of them. But the young people of color and first-generation students that I know have endured more than most because they've *had* to.

As one of my former colleagues once said, "These students aren't entitled. If anything, I wish they asked for *more*." They've survived crappy educations, reduced economic opportunities, discrimination, and on and on. The ones who make it to college are superhuman. They show up for class after pulling an overnight shift at an assisted-living facility; they never ask for extensions or favors; they don't complain, even when their instructor shows up to class drunk/high or falls asleep in the middle of class. (This has all happened. I wish I were making it up.)

Entitlement is learned. And to be entitled is to believe you deserve certain things. We live in a culture where some of us are held to impossible standards—women, people of color, survivors of sexual assault, the poor, immigrants, Dreamers—just to be seen as human. But all of us deserve to be treated with dignity and respect, even if we are not extraordinary. Even if we are not perfect.

* * *

It's easy to default to the stories we've been told our entire lives. As a child, I learned a certain story about myself, gleaned from nursery rhymes and history books, dolls and bad jokes, pop culture and media. I believed I was not precious or worthy but a punch line and a punching bag, a thing to abuse, not cherish. According to Chimamanda Ngozi Adichie, that's precisely the danger of a single story, with its pernicious ability to rob individuals of their dignity and reduce them to a stereotype. The only way I could undo this damage, this brainwashing, was to read *different* stories—stories I found in books, in art, in music, in friendship. And I couldn't stop there. I also had to start *telling* different stories, not just to myself, but to my children and my students.

Stories are not set in stone. If we look to oral storytelling traditions, we learn that telling stories is a collective endeavor, a way to pass on cultural knowledge from one generation to the next. It's social, based on dialogue and connection between storyteller and audience. It's dynamic, offering room for improvisation and adaptation based on the setting and the individual quirks of the storyteller. Each generation gets to choose what stories to pass on, and those stories tell us who we are and what we value. Stories are living things. Humans evolve and values change. So should our stories.

I'm choosing to tell my daughter old stories but also new ones. One day, she, too, will get to choose which stories to pass on. I think that's the greatest legacy I can give her—the ability to decide for herself what she wants to keep, what she wants to tweak, and, finally, what she wants to create anew.

My daughter is now thirteen years old, the same age I was when I first began to rebel against my mother. I won't lie—I'm terrified. If she's even one-tenth as defiant or rageful as I was, I might die.

But then I think, *Stop it, Julia.* We're not doomed to repeat the past, nor are we obligated to repeat the same narratives of suffering and victimization. My daughter may have inherited the shadow of depression and anxiety, but she has also inherited the gift of language, of art, of music. I watch her embrace these ways to restore her soul and restore her humanity, and I wonder if that, too, is a blessing from her ancestors. There's intergenerational healing in my family, not just intergenerational trauma.

What's more, my daughter *is supposed to* rebel. She's supposed to separate and individuate, to become her own person. I'm her mother, not her master. She is not eternally obligated to obey me. While filial piety can be virtuous, it can also become a trap, keeping subsequent generations in a state of eternal subordination. In this way, it shares the same paternalistic logic as institutions like slavery and colonialism. The slave master is a benevolent father who feeds and clothes his enslaved "children." The colonizer is a benevolent savior who takes up the burden of civilizing the "savages." How dare the enslaved or colonized protest their mistreatment? Their job is to be eternally grateful and submissive, a perpetually obedient child.

To my daughter, I say: you must bite the hand that feeds you—even if that hand is mine. I'm reminded of Jamaica Kincaid's novels, in which she demonstrates how the relationship between West Indian mothers and daughters eerily re-creates the relationship between colonizer and colonized, between "Mother England" and Daughter Colony. As the daughter grows older, she rebels against her mother's strictures of how a young woman must behave and act. Her mother, in turn, sees her as treacherous, a thankless child. Yet the daughter *must* resist in order to become her own person. Remaining under her mother's thumb is akin to perpetual subjugation.

Honoring your parents does not mean submitting to authoritarian rule and perpetual servitude. Nor does it mean stifling critique or dissent. And this doesn't apply just to filial piety in East Asian cultures or paternalism in colonial and postcolonial contexts. It also applies to the founding ideals of this country.

We Americans are taught to revere our Founding Fathers, rebels themselves who sought freedom from British tyranny and declared that "all men are created equal." I am grateful to live in a country that espouses these values. But I also recognize that our Founding Fathers were white, slave-owning men who did not uphold these ideals in their own lives and certainly did not see me—an Asian woman—as their "equal." Does this make me a traitor? Or someone who sees the Founding Fathers as flawed human beings?

I've bitten the hand that fed me, whether that hand was that of a parent, a teacher, a college, a nation. I'm grateful for my upbringing, but that doesn't mean I must be eternally beholden to those who raised, educated, and governed me. I'm not a horse who must be broken by its master. Nor am I a wayward child who needs a firm, controlling hand. I've grown up. I have certain inalienable rights to Life, Liberty, and the Pursuit of Happiness. Don't dehumanize or infantilize me.

And now, my daughter is starting to push back and pull away, to assert her own independence. It's a disconcerting experience, being on the other side, realizing I'm now the authority figure who must be resisted. I can't say I like it, but I remind himself that she's growing up, discovering that I'm not infallible, asserting her own identity. This isn't a betrayal (sob). That's what I try to tell myself, at least. Check with me again in a few years.

* * *

In the early months of my daughter's life, my mother and I spent more time together than we had in years. She would drop by with miyukgook or groceries from Koreatown, and I'd beg for her to stay longer. She would tell me I had no idea what I was doing and that my daughter was fussy because I was eating the wrong things and also I had to wear socks all the time and stop drinking anything cold and aigo, what in the world would I do without her? Then she would leave to hit the sales at Goodwill or take a Zumba class at the YMCA and I'd wonder, *Why can't she be the kind of halmoni who wants to spend time with her grandkids full-time? Can't she see I'm dying?*

"I'm busy," my mom would say when I asked her to babysit. "I have things I want to do."

"Holy shit," I told my sister. "I think Mom has become *Americanized.*"

As my daughter grew older and I'd try to discipline her, my mother would step in and tell me *I* was being too harsh. Once, while my parents were visiting me in Las Vegas, my daughter, then four years old, dragged her one-year-old brother down the stairs and split his chin open. I panicked when I saw blood and chin fat spilling out of the wound. "YOU'RE IN SO MUCH TROUBLE," I yelled at my daughter as she cowered behind her grandmother. "I'll deal with you later."

We took my son to Urgent Care, where the nurse tried and failed to strap my son to a "medical papoose" so he could glue the wound shut. Flustered, the nurse sent us to the ER, where the doctor perfunctorily superglued my son's chin, all the while complaining that this was a waste of his time and should have been handled by Urgent Care. We got home past midnight.

My mother was waiting up for us.

"Where is she?" I asked.

"Asleep," my mom said. "Don't bother her."

"I'm going to kill her," I said. "We *told* her not to rough-house with her brother. She never listens."

"No. Don't yell at her. She's sorry."

"I'll punish her in the morning."

"No punishment! You're too hard on her!"

I looked at my mother, incredulous. "You were so much harder on me when I was a kid! All you did was scream and yell!"

"I want my granddaughter to love me," she said.

"But you didn't want *me* to love you?"

"It's different. You needed the discipline."

"You nearly killed us."

My mother was quiet for a moment.

"Remember the time you threw a fork at your sister?" she now asked.

I cringed, feeling a wave of shame.

"It was my fault," I said. "I was a total monster. I could have blinded her."

My mother looked at me and said, "No, it was my fault."

"How was it your fault?" I asked. I was shocked. My mother *never* apologizes, and for a second, I felt all my old resentment and self-righteous rage well up. It *was* her fault. My mom lost her temper all the time and went physical. I was just mimicking the behavior I saw around me. Thank *God* she was finally taking responsibility. *She* was the monster, not me.

"It was my fault you and your sister were fighting," she said.

"What were we fighting about?" I asked. "I can't even remember."

"You were fighting over food," my mom said.

"Food? What do you mean?"

"I was trying to save money, so I made only one package of ramen and I told you two to share it. You were hungry. You were fighting because you wanted more to eat. That's why you threw the fork at your sister."

I couldn't speak. One package of ramen was twenty-five cents. My sister and I were teenagers then. Were we really that poor? I had no idea.

"I should have made another package," my mom was saying. "I was trying to save every single penny." She paused. "Don't be too hard on your daughter. It's not worth it."

Chapter Fourteen

KINFOLK

When I was in college, the head of my dormitory (then called a "master") was a white philosophy professor who had been a Freedom Rider in the 1960s. His family traced its roots back to the *Mayflower*, and he was educated at elite boarding schools and universities in America and Europe. As a young man, he'd rebelled against the WASP values of his forebears by joining antiwar protests and becoming an avowed atheist, and now, at the age of sixty, he'd become one of those crunchy New England liberals who wore Patagonia fleeces and Birkenstocks and looked a lot like Bernie Sanders.

Like many white radicals and hippies from the 1960s, this professor seemed confident in his countercultural and antiracist bona fides. He oversaw a racially diverse group of student advisers whose job it was to help first- and second-year students with everything from roommate conflict to academic struggles, mental health issues, sexual assault, and much, much more. Half of the group were designated "minority affairs advisers" and tasked with educating students on issues of race, ethnicity, and other minoritized identities. We talked a lot about issues of diversity and inclusion in these meetings, and this professor would often bring up what he saw was a central flaw in our discussions.

"When students ask for more diversity, what they really mean is that they want more people who look like themselves," he would argue, pausing to let that sink in. I heard him say this more than once, to different groups of people. He was never challenged, partly because he was an older, white man in a position of authority, but also because he was what we considered an "ally." He'd "marched with King," as so many older white progressives liked to say. Years later, when scrolling through the comments on a *New York Times* article, I saw this same professor quoted by a reader who agreed with his premise that the push for diversity isn't really diverse—that it was actually just different identity groups trying to further their own interests in what was sneeringly referred to as "identity politics."

I should have spoken up back then, but I was young and insecure. Moreover, I *liked* this professor. *He must know something I don't*, I thought. As I got older, though, I kept encountering versions of this thinking—if not this exact argument—among my older, white, so-called progressive colleagues. It was a version of the zero-sum, scarcity culture mentality baked into white supremacist culture. The assumption was always that people of color thought the way white people thought, that someone's gain was inevitably someone else's loss. It's the logic of settler colonialism, slavery, and capitalism: the white colonist's gain (land, human ownership, resources) was Indigenous and Black people's loss (relationships to land and culture, sovereignty, freedom).

When my professor referred to students who "ask for more diversity," he was referring to nonwhite students. He presumed white students wouldn't be the ones asking for more diversity, because there were plenty of people who looked like them around campus. According to his logic, Black people would want more Black people around, Indigenous people would want more Indigenous people around, Asian people would want more Asian people around, and on and on, each purely out for their own racial/ethnic group's interests. Inevitably, this would lead to less room for white people, which is why they were the ones uninterested in—and sometimes hostile to—"diversity."

I cannot express how flawed this reasoning is. We are a multiracial, multiethnic nation. If I were solely concerned with having more Asian people around, I'd move to Korea and promote ethnic nationalism. But I don't want to live in a monoracial or monoethnic country. How fucking boring. I want to see people who look like me, but also people who look different from me. I want more Indigenous people and Black people and Latinx people to access spaces historically foreclosed to them—not just more Asian people. And while I know there are white people who just want more white people around, I know there are others who don't want to live in a monoracial bubble.

Today, this professor would be rightfully accused of whitesplaining and mansplaining. But he's not alone or even unusual in presuming to know what people of color really want. Many white progressives don't realize how thoroughly they've absorbed white supremacist ideology and paternalism in their thinking and actions. They still center whiteness. They still default to Us/Them thinking.

They still think of "diversity" as adding a little color to a white base, or as a lazy synonym for "BIPOC." This professor's *official job title* was "master of the college." We were all ostensibly part of one big multicultural family, but it was clear who was really in charge.

* * *

In 2018, I attended an academic conference where every talk was preceded by a land acknowledgment, where the men and women's bathrooms were renamed "all-gender" bathrooms, and where speakers introduced themselves with their racial/ethnic/sexual identity and their preferred pronouns. I won't lie. I thought it was performative B.S. I complained about it to my friend Jane, who is Taos Pueblo and an emeritus professor of Indigenous literature. Jane, to her credit, patiently listened to me. But as I was speaking to her, I realized how intolerant I sounded, how much I was centering my own experiences of "how things should be," advocating for the same kind of willful forgetting of our nation's past that I so raged against when it came to historical injustices like American slavery or Japanese American incarceration. I was basically suggesting that Indigenous people, gender nonbinary people, and people with marginalized identities shouldn't have a *right* to be so vocal or visible—that they should just get over it. With a shock, I realized I was telling *myself* that I didn't have a right to be so vocal or visible—that *I* should just get over it.

I grew up in the Catholic Church—the religious arm of the Spanish settler-colonial enterprise—absorbing lessons that boys should be boys, girls should be girls, and homosexuality was a sin. I believed Father Junípero Serra was a saint (before he was literally made one by Pope Francis) who helped found the California missions and convert the native population. I even wrote a hagiographic book report about Serra in the third grade, which I got to read over the school PA system. I learned nothing about Indigenous history, very little about colonialism or slavery, and had almost no exposure to Black history, queer history, or my own history. I just took that as the norm. Thirty years later, I'd educated myself in Black history, was totally on board with gay rights, and supported Dreamers and undocumented immigrants. I thought I was pretty hot shit.

But I wasn't. My brain had calcified. I was resistant to change. Gender pronouns puzzled me. Land acknowledgments confused me. My immediate response was to react like lots of people do—blame it on woke culture run amok or mock how cringingly earnest my colleagues were. It was always other people's fault that I felt uncomfortable—not mine. Yet what did it cost me to listen to a land acknowledgment, or use an all-gender bathroom, or use someone's preferred pronouns? *Nothing* except my own complacency. What I gained was a recognition that we were on Paiute land that had been stolen by white settlers and turned into Las Vegas, that all-gender bathrooms were just bathrooms, and that using preferred pronouns acknowledged a person's gender identity *and* humanity. In the past few years, as these practices have spread beyond academia, I'm reminded of how quickly cultural attitudes can change, even for curmudgeons like me. Concepts that had seemed absurd to me not that long ago now seemed like basic acts of human dignity and recognition.

I had to decolonize my mind. I use the word "decolonization" because antiracism too often perpetuates a white-Black, racist-antiracist binary. The focus on anti-Black racism is necessary and urgent, but the language of the antiracism industry centers a white person trying to become less fragile and more empathetic. I choose the word decolonization because it is rooted specifically in *settler* colonialism—the extermination and replacement of Indigenous peoples with a new society of white European settlers—that paved the way for the trafficking and enslavement of African people and the establishment of our white supremacist society in which anyone "nonwhite"—such as "Indian," "Oriental," "Mexican," "Negro"—is inferior.* As Eve Tuck and K. Wayne Yang point out, decolonization is not a metaphor or a synonym for social justice. It is to stand in solidarity with Indigenous peoples, to return stewardship of land, to offer reparations. It is another step to decentering whiteness and reframing our relationship to one another.

Decolonizing my mind means recognizing that even the Black-white binary I take as fact, the one that makes me feel invisible or tertiary, is a white supremacist construct built on the annihilation of Indigenous lives and the dispossession of Indigenous land. I was born on land inhabited by the Gabrielino-Tongva people for thousands of years. That land was colonized by the Spanish, who converted, enslaved, and killed the Indigenous caretakers. That land was then annexed by the United States, a white supremacist nation settled by the British, Dutch, Spanish,

---

* "Ethnic" white people (Irish, Jewish, Italian, and so on) have historically suffered religious oppression and discrimination in the United States, but have since "assimilated into whiteness."

and French, who conquered or decimated or enslaved or "removed" countless Indigenous tribes (the Pequot, the Ottawa, the Pueblo Indians, the Cherokee, the Shawnee, the Seminole, and more); who trafficked and enslaved countless African peoples (Mende, Temne, Hausa, Igbo, and more); who systematically segregated, excluded, and expelled Asian peoples (Chinese, Japanese, Indian, "Orientals," and more); who "intervened" in Central America (Panama, Nicaragua, El Salvador, Honduras, and more), the Caribbean (Haiti, Cuba, Puerto Rico), and Asia (Korea, Vietnam, Philippines), creating mass numbers of refugees, migrants, displaced peoples. Which is how my family ended up immigrating here, settling first on Lenape land (Philadelphia), then moving cross-country to settle "permanently" on Gabrielino-Tongva land (Los Angeles basin). My grandfather and grandmother, *my* ancestors, are now buried in Whittier, on the sacred land of Tongva ancestors.

This is my history, too. And it is a history that demands I stop centering whiteness and instead center an Indigenous perspective, to consider the ways in which I, too, have been willfully ignorant about this country's past. What does it mean that my friend Jane, while walking through Chicago O'Hare airport, was told, "Go back to your own country" by a white woman? If this is anyone's country, it is Jane's. And the white passerby? It is she who is the uninvited visitor, the settler, the interloper. It is I who am the uninvited visitor, the settler, the interloper. If anyone should be cast out, it is us. This land is *not* my land. This land is *not* your land. Claiming an American identity, as I do, is an act of breathtaking entitlement.

"See me as an American," I ask. But not at the expense of seeing Indigenous people and their history. This was Indigenous land before this was white supremacist country. As Viet Thanh Nguyen writes, "If we belong to this country, then this country belongs to us, every part of it, including its systemic anti-Black racism and its colonization of Indigenous peoples and land." This, too, is my history. This, too, is my heritage.

* * *

Like the identity categories of "Black/African American," "Hispanic/Latinx," and "Asian American," the term "Native American/American Indian" is a legacy of white supremacy. It encompasses many different sovereign nations, clan affiliations, traditions, religions, regions held together by a common experience of European colonization, genocide, and discrimination. Kim Weaver (Lakota) writes, "There was no native American identity prior to contact with Europeans." You were Ojibwe or you were Diné or you were Oglala until you were told by Christopher Columbus/white settlers that you were "Indian," a misnomer that was later euphemized/modified to Native American/Canadian, or Amerindian, or American Indian.

As a child, I assumed Native Americans were a vast, undifferentiated mass of savages that included the "Injuns" I read about in the Little House on the Prairie books, the Indians who broke bread with the Pilgrims on Thanksgiving, and the Indians who were converted by Father Serra at the California Missions. I did not realize that the Ingalls family was squatting on Osage land, that the Wampanoags were later slaughtered in a bloody colonial war, and that

Father Serra abused and enslaved the Gabrielino, Ohlone, Chumash, and many other Indigenous tribes. I'd absorbed the colonial myths, just like I was supposed to. I saw myself as Laura Ingalls or the Pilgrims or Father Serra; I saw Native Americans as a mythical lump of inhumanity. What I did not realize is that according to the white imaginary, I was not Laura Ingalls; I was actually part of that mythical lump of inhumanity, the other.

Today, Indigenous is the self-determined, politically and historically distinct term used to refer to the First Peoples of North America (First Nations, Métis, Inuit), American Indian, Alaska Native, Hawaiian/Kānaka Maoli peoples in United States–occupied territories, and *indio* peoples in land colonized by the Spanish and now called Mexico. Daniel Heath Justice (Cherokee) writes that Indigenous peoples share "a relation to the land, the ancestors, and the kinship networks, lifeways, and languages that originated in this hemisphere and continue in often besieged but always resilient forms." This is not to ignore the specificity and complexity of each individual tribal nation or to suggest Indigenous peoples are a monolith. This is about connection even in difference.

I especially don't want to fall into the trap of fetishizing Indigenous culture the way whiteness fetishizes so many nonwhite cultures. It's gross and reductive. But discussions around Indigenous culture and identity have helped me decenter whiteness in profound ways. It has allowed me to see the ways in which my own Korean heritage shares a respect for elders and ancestors and a devotion to the collective good that, while sometimes hierarchical and conformist, can also be a source of love and community. It has taught me another way out of the quandary of race in this country and helped me rediscover what it means to be human.

How do we behave as good relatives? How do we become good ancestors? How do we learn to live together? These are among the questions Daniel Heath Justice asks, and these are the questions that are facing all of us as we confront a world riven by hate, scarcity, poverty, climate change, inequality, and violence. We have forgotten how to be human. We have forgotten our relationship with the land and water, with the animal world, with each other. We have overvalued individual gain over the collective good, left our children a shit sandwich as their inheritance, hoarded and extracted and exhausted resources. We have been partitioned into races and nations and pitted against one another in an existential death match.

I always imagined family and kinship according to narrow definitions constructed by white supremacist (and, to a lesser extent, Korean nationalist) notions of blood and racial purity. In the United States, this thinking was behind antimiscegenation laws (which criminalized racial mixing), the "one-drop rule" (the notion that if you had even one drop of "Negro" blood, you were classified as "Negro"), and eugenics/white supremacy (which saw its gruesome apotheosis in Hitler's Final Solution). In Korea, this thinking was behind ethnic nationalism (Koreans as a race descended from a single ancestor, united in history, culture, and identity against Japanese colonialism), blood purity (pride in ethnic homogeneity and hostility toward racial mixing), and patrilineal blood culture (no children out of wedlock, no mixed-race children or adopted children allowed).

I've witnessed this from both sides. When I was in middle school, one of my white friends invited me on a ski trip to Big Bear with her church youth group. On the van ride there, a white girl in her group criticized intermarriage, telling me she thought Asian people should marry Asian people, and white people should marry white people. I barely understood what my sexual identity was at that time, much less what kind of person I wanted to marry—or if I even *wanted* to get married—and yet I understood she was policing white racial purity and saw me as a threat.

Many years later, I was visiting Korea with my parents and met one of my cousins, who spent the entire visit explaining to me that pure-blooded Koreans should marry pure-blooded Koreans, and all other races were inferior—though Leonardo DiCaprio was a marginally acceptable white guy. I have heard countless stories of Korean parents who disapprove of or even disown their children for dating or marrying someone non-Korean. I've seen the way "pure-blood" Korean people look askance at mixed-race Koreans, or Korean adoptees, or even the children of divorced parents. I understood they were policing Korean ethnic purity and saw non-Koreans and half-Koreans and "illegitimate" Koreans and diasporic Koreans—gyopo like me, who have lost touch with our roots, our language, our culture—as a threat.

So when I began to read more about kinship in Indigenous culture, I realized that the whole notion of blood, race, and purity were inherently problematic. In the white American context, concepts like blood and race have been used to preserve white supremacy while subordinating all other groups. During the antebellum period, the "one-drop rule" conveniently expanded the pool of enslaved Black labor, including the children of white slave owners and enslaved women. During World War II, anyone with "one drop of Japanese blood" who lived on the West Coast was incarcerated as a potential traitor—including orphaned infants! In the case of Indigenous peoples, the notion of blood purity was used to systematically deny treaty rights and claim ownership of Indigenous land. According to the perverse logic of blood quantum, one drop of Native American blood was *not* sufficient to make you Native American (and therefore entitled to federal benefits). In this case, it was in white supremacy's interest to *deny* Indigenous heritage, and thus Indigenous peoples were forced to quantify their blood, with the eventual goal of "breeding out" or assimilating them into whiteness completely.

Sometimes one drop of nonwhite blood makes you nonwhite (Black, Asian), except when one drop of nonwhite blood makes you white (thus extinguishing Indigenous identity and rights). If you're confused, get in line. This is the perverse and ruthless logic of white supremacy.

When I would work myself into contortions over the byzantine rules of race and racial identity in this country, my friend Jane would gently point out that for Indigenous peoples, race and ethnicity are ultimately white supremacist and colonial constructs. Indigenous identity emerges from an alternate understanding of sovereign nationhood, kinship, and belonging. Niigaanwewidam Sinclair (Anishinaabe) writes, "Being Indigenous has a little to do with blood and ancestry, but has far more to do with the relationships one builds and embodies." When people like Elizabeth Warren and Blake Lively claim Cherokee blood, they are defining Indigeneity according to the rules of whiteness. But Indigenous identity is about so much more than drops of blood or snippets of DNA, which too often reduce human beings to spurious math equations.

How does it feel to be broken into parts? You are 5/8 Indian. You are 1/16 Indian. You are 3/32 Indian. Always, always, you are considered a fraction of a whole, less than a full human, insufficient, a breed like a horse or a dog. This same bad math—the math of white supremacy—was behind the Three-Fifths clause in the American Constitution, which allowed southern states to inflate their congressional representation by counting enslaved Black people as three-fifths the number of white inhabitants in the state (while still denying them citizenship rights). This was not about recognizing Black people as human. This was about cooking the books. Black people were convenient fractions, three-fifths of a white person when it benefited white supremacy, zero-fifths of a white person when it didn't.

People like to say numbers don't lie or that math is objective, but numbers and math have been used to perpetuate injustice *all the time.* Don't like the answer? Just move some numbers around, change the variables, run a Ponzi scheme, gerrymander districts, transfer money to an offshore account. Take a DNA test like Elizabeth Warren did and claim the results show you are 1/164 to 1/1024 Cherokee, and then express surprise when the Cherokee Nation responds "we don't know her," because numbers are too often used by the white majority to inform minoritized peoples who counts and who doesn't. Warren made the same mistake as lots of us in positions of privilege do—*presuming* belonging, *assuming* acceptance. But as Kim TallBear (Sisseton Wahpeton Oyate) writes, "[Indigenous peoples] construct belonging and citizenship in ways that do not consider these genetic ancestry tests. So it's not just a matter of what you claim, but it's a matter of who claims you."

What a radical idea! In this country, I've been taught that it's all about naming and claiming, the quintessential colonial act, the power move. Christopher Columbus showed up and claimed Quisqueya and Ayiti for Spain, renaming it Hispaniola; Captain Cook showed up and claimed the Hawaiian islands for England, renaming them the Sandwich Islands; Samuel de Champlain showed up and claimed Algonquin, Inuit, and Iroquois land for France, renaming it Québec. But the relationship was not reciprocal or mutual. It was colonial and imperial. It was nonconsensual.

I am not Columbus, Cook, or Champlain, but I've been trying to wedge myself into this colonial and imperial world they created by relying on the language of naming and claiming. I *claim* I am American, I *claim* I am Asian American, I *claim* that I am a person of color. I am mimicking the language of power, naming myself and staking my claim. For years, I sought belonging in spaces that did not always reciprocate—school, work, America. I attempted to infiltrate these colonial and imperial spaces. "I belong here!" I screamed. "I am a citizen! I am an American! I am human!"

But who claims me? What community do I belong to, and do they see me as one of them? It's not white supremacist America, who provisionally accepts me only when I am useful to them and expels me when I am not. It is not necessarily the Korean community, who may see me as deracinated and Americanized, though we may share "blood." I joke about how I feel like an orphan, a bastard stepchild, a bad American and a bad Korean, an imperfect fit wherever I go. It is only recently—really, within the last five years—that I have finally found a community of women of color and accomplices whom I claim and who also claim me.

In recent years, it's become common to use pop psychology phrases like "finding your tribe" and "finding your people," colonialist constructions that reduce Indigenous ways of belonging into cheesy metaphors. Joining a knitting club or subscribing to a corporate brand are not Indigenous acts. Indigenous belonging is a specific thing: the rights of sovereign nations to determine for themselves whom they claim as members. In the same way I do not want to fetishize Indigenous culture, I also do not want to appropriate Indigenous cultural practices. Rather, I want to step back and consider how Indigenous precepts of reciprocity and mutuality can help us better understand our web of relationships and connections outside of a white supremacist framework.

There's a phrase that has been attributed to Zora Neale Hurston—"All skinfolk ain't kinfolk." Just because someone shares your racial identity does not mean they're your friend or have your best interests at heart. The American racial system loves slotting us into demographic categories and then expressing surprise when we don't act as one monolithic entity. There are Americans of Asian descent who share my racial and ethnic identity, but whose politics or worldviews I abhor. I have met Americans of Asian descent who are agents of white supremacy or ethnic supremacy or patriarchy. They are not my kin. I do not claim them, and they do not claim me. The kinship I claim, and that I hope claims me, is one that moves beyond narrow notions of blood and skin color to gesture toward a broader understanding of humanity as articulated by Indigenous understandings of consensus and connection.

As my student Yoán once said to me, the quintessential decolonial act can be boiled down to: "be a human to the human in front of you."

Who are my kin? They are Indigenous, they are Black, they are Asian, they are Latinx, they are women, they are nonbinary, they are queer, they are immigrants, they are working-class and poor, they are white allies and accomplices—they are anyone who has felt the sharp sting of bigotry and hate. They believe in collective action and mutual care while respecting individual agency. They do not have to be related to me by blood or share my ethnic heritage; they do not have to be American. They are my family, and I am theirs. Just as all skinfolk ain't kinfolk, all kinfolk ain't skinfolk.

The historian Benedict Anderson describes nations as "imagined communities," a way for disparate peoples to visualize themselves as part of a group. What connects someone like me to a Latina grandmother in Nevada, to a Mennonite farmer in Ohio, to a young Black child in Florida? Nothing, really, but a belief that we are all Americans, with an imaginary, shared belief in abstract ideals like equality, democracy, and liberty. It's a nice fantasy, but it is always on the brink of cracking up because too many of us disagree on what "American" *really* means, and whom it includes. Too many of us have limited imaginations.

What if we come up with a different imagined community, a version of Martin Luther King, Jr.'s "beloved community," a community of care, of kinfolk who share a belief in our collective humanity? No haters allowed. Just a commitment to being good ancestors and good relatives and good people. Understanding that the relationship is consensual and dynamic, based on communion, not domination. Recognizing we are imperfect and will fail, but that we will keep getting up and trying again. I know it's a fantasy, but so, too, is America. Maybe we need to imagine bigger, beyond nation, beyond race, beyond ethnicity, just beyond.

One of the most beautiful words I've learned is "survivance." Developed by Gerald Vizenor (Anishinaabe), survivance is central to understanding Indigenous lifeways. Some consider it a portmanteau of "survival" and "endurance," or "survival" and "resistance," but I like to think of it as a blending of "survival" and "vibrance." Indigenous peoples have survived unspeakable oppression at the hands of colonial powers, but they refuse to let white supremacy define them as victims. They are not tragic. They are not inferior. They have not vanished. They are creators, storytellers, artists, visionaries. They are here, and they are showing us the way forward.

My dear friend Jane is Taos Pueblo. Her ancestors lived for over a thousand years on sacred land near the Rio Grande River in what is today known as New Mexico. Taos Pueblo was a place of connection and exchange, where Indigenous peoples from the Great Plains and along the Rio Grande met to trade and share information. In 1540, Spanish conquistadors arrived, followed by Catholic missionaries, imposing their religion, government, and language on the Taos peoples. The Taos peoples resisted this cultural incursion; they rose up against the Spanish colonizers, burning down the church not once but twice. In response, the Spanish massacred, enslaved, and mutilated the Pueblo Indians.

But Taos Pueblo never stopped resisting. They rose up when Spain ceded their land to Mexico in 1821; they rose up again when Mexico ceded their land to the United States in 1847. They resisted when their children were forcibly removed and assimilated into white culture at boarding schools like Carlisle Indian Industrial School in Pennsylvania, where the reigning motto was "Kill the Indian, save the man." They preserved their ancient dwellings, their rituals, their sacred history in the face of Spanish, Mexican, and American invasion. In 1970, they successfully regained stewardship of forty-six thousand acres of sacred land around Blue Lake stolen by the United States government at the turn of the century.

The Taos Pueblo community still thrives and still tells its story. Jane is a living embodiment of this—she is a connector, an educator, a storyteller. She's taught me how to be a good human, a good relation, a good ancestor, and a good friend. And when I want to give up or die of despair, she is there to tell me, "We [Indigenous peoples] are living lives of survivance. And so are you."

Chapter Fifteen

WE, TOO

I have a very common name, something I'm reminded of every time I go to CVS to pick up a prescription and the pharmacist pulls up a list of fifty Julia Lees within a five-mile radius. Search for me on social media and you'll find a million Julia Lees, of all different races and ethnicities. Probably the most famous Julia Lee in America is a Black woman, a dirty blues singer from Kansas City who had a string of R&B hits in the 1940s (among them "King Size Papa" and "Snatch and Grab It"). There's a white, blond Julia Lee who appeared in episodes of *Angel* in the early 2000s. There's also a Julia Lee who I joke is my doppelgänger because she is around my age, of Korean descent, and also a college professor in the Los Angeles area (her specialty is Asian American literature, but she also studies African American literature). The doubling is almost uncanny. The "other" Julia Lee (as I call her) uses her middle initial, H., which stands for "Hyun-Joo." Hyun-Joo is my sister's Korean name (mine is Sun-Joo). I joke that we might be related.

I once met the other Julia Lee when I interviewed for

a job at a large state university in the Southwest. She had just been hired to teach Asian American literature, and I was up for a job in Victorian literature. We met for lunch and laughed uncomfortably about how weird it was to meet each other. Other professors made awkward jokes that it would be impossibly confusing to have two Julia Lees in the same department. (I thought it would actually make their lives easier, because they would inevitably mistake the two of us for each other, anyway.) They needn't have worried because I did not get the job.

I used to resent having such a common name, especially when I was young and coming up. I desperately wanted to be seen as an individual, as one-of-a-kind. Having one of the most common last names in the world, along with a first name that was also fairly common (and frequently misspelled "Julie") meant that I often met people who would exclaim, "Oh! How funny! I know another Julia Lee!" For a while, I used my Korean name as my middle name to professionally distinguish myself from the "other" Julia Lee. She was Julia H. Lee, and I was Julia Sun-Joo Lee. That was the name I published under early in my academic career. (I stopped using it after learning that a Chinese American classmate claimed I was using my Korean middle name to signal my ethnicity, and thus to secure jobs as a diversity hire. You just can't win.)

Now I go by Julia Lee, partly because it's my legal name (I have no official middle name; Sun-Joo is the name my grandfather gave me), partly because of shame (see above), and partly because I actually *like* having a common name. It's harder to find me. I can choose to disappear if I want. I feel a sense of kinship with my fellow Julia Lees. I used to get emails intended for the other Julia Lee—requests to review manuscripts, invitations to apply for jobs—and sometimes I'd feel bad because I was the wrong Julia Lee, and the other Julia Lee was clearly *killing* it professionally. But then I'd realize I was being stupid and perpetuating the white supremacist mindset that there can only be one. There is room for lots of Julia Lees. Our name is a point of connection, not cancellation. I am proud of her, even *honored* to be mistaken for her. People who search "Julia Lee" online will find thousands of us, living all over the world, representing all sorts of different backgrounds, doing all kinds of different things. I think that's rad. It's an honor just to be Julia Lee.

* * *

Growing up in Columbia, Missouri, the Korean American filmmaker Grace Lee was used to being one of few Asian Americans in her predominantly white community, the only Grace Lee around. That sense of uniqueness dissipated when she moved to cities like Los Angeles and New York, places with large Asian American populations where, to her chagrin, she discovered she was one in a vast sea of Grace Lees. Everyone knew someone named Grace Lee, and that other Grace Lee seemed like an utterly generic caricature of the model minority: a nice, smart, petite Asian girl who played the piano and studied a lot.

I went to school with two Grace Lees, both from Korean families. One was the daughter of a pastor, who named her Eun He, which loosely translates to "grace" or "favor." The other was a year above me in school and now works as a lawyer in London. I've been called Grace. A few years ago,

I tore my ACL, and the white medic who was helping me asked my name before proceeding to call me Grace while she treated me. I didn't correct her because I was in too much pain, and also because I found it kind of hilarious. I was an honorary Grace Lee—I fit the model minority stereotype of a nice, petite Asian girl, a figment of white supremacy's imagination. It didn't matter what my actual name was—we were all the same generic person.

That tension between individual identity and generic stereotype is something many of us struggle with. We're already considered faceless, homogeneous, and inter-changeable by the white imaginary; even our names seem to invite this with their sameness—surnames like Lee, Wang, Nguyen; Americanized first names like Grace, Jean, Jane. All look the same; all named the same. Raised in this country, where individuality and originality are prized and fetishized, we feel doubly doomed to invisibility. (This reminds me of the time I worked as a personal assistant to an aging white screenwriter and former D-list actress whose last name was also Lee. When she handed me my first paycheck, it was made out to Julia Kim. You cannot make this up.)

But what if we reject the white gaze? What if we see beauty and solidarity, rather than blandness and uniformity, in our names and our cultures? What if we see *power* in our abundance? The filmmaker Grace Lee, initially frustrated by the racist banality of the Grace Lee stereotype, decided to interview other Grace Lees, in the process discovering that the name Grace Lee contains multitudes. There's a Grace Lee who is a newscaster in Hawaii, a Grace Lee who makes voodoo dolls, Grace Lees who fit the stereotype and Grace Lees who defy it. There's an entire network of Graces out there, connected by a name that itself speaks of connection.

Through her research, the filmmaker Grace Lee ultimately met Grace Lee Boggs, the legendary Chinese American civil rights activist who worked ceaselessly for Black liberation. This Grace Lee was born above her father's Chinese restaurant in Providence, Rhode Island, in 1915 and grew up in New York City, in a predominantly white neighborhood where anti-Asian racism was rampant and mundane. Although she earned a PhD in philosophy from Bryn Mawr in 1940, she knew no university would hire someone like her, a woman of Chinese descent, so she moved to Chicago, where she met C. L. R. James, the great Trinidadian Marxist and intellectual, and began working on behalf of the Black community. In 1953, she married Jimmy Boggs, a Black auto worker and fellow activist, and they spent the next several decades organizing in the Detroit community, participating in the civil rights movement, the women's movement, the Asian American movement, the labor movement. The FBI's COINTELPRO couldn't figure her out, speculating that she was likely "Afro-Chinese." In their limited imaginations, why else would a woman of Asian descent be so involved in Black organizing?

Grace Lees were not supposed to be radicals. They were not supposed to hang out with Malcolm X. They were definitely not supposed to form cross-racial coalitions and inspire a new generation of Asian American activists. And yet Grace Lee Boggs recognized that her race and gender were inextricably linked to her political identity. "Had I not been born female and Chinese American," she writes in her memoir,

"I would not have realized from early on that fundamental changes were necessary in our society. Had I not been born female and Chinese American, I might have ended up teaching philosophy at a university, an observer rather than a participant in the humanity-stretching movements that have defined the last half of the twentieth century." Boggs may have been an outsider, but her marginalized status allowed her insight and even unexpected opportunity. It was precisely *because* she was Asian American and a woman that she could critique conversations around race and gender, pushing future activists to think beyond Black-white binaries or to question the masculinist and hierarchical tendencies of movement work.

What I love most about Grace Lee Boggs is that she exemplifies a model of Asian American leadership that sees our imagined "weaknesses," our supposed "niceness" and "meekness," as strengths. Boggs acknowledges that she has a "habit of self-effacement" that makes something like self-promotion—or writing a memoir—extremely difficult for her. As the daughter of Chinese immigrants, she was taught "to think of myself in relation to others, rather than as an individual." Yet these are the very traits critical to future social justice work, work that must be grounded in reciprocity and communion, not ego, hierarchy, and inequality. Boggs favors collaboration over confrontation, asking questions over providing answers. Asian American women already know how to do this; we have been doing it our entire lives. Our leadership may look different from white male leadership, but that does not make it any less powerful.

Boggs died in 2015 at the age of one hundred, but I see her legacy everywhere. I see it in the growing number of multiracial coalitions led by women of color and committed to collective action and change. I see it in the way Black and Asian American activists have stood together in the face of anti-Black and anti-Asian hate. I see it in the way the Latinx/Chicanx movement, the Indigenous movement, the LGBTQ+ movement, the Disability Rights movement, and more are "humanity-stretching movements" that ask us to look beyond the narrow scope of our own individual identity. For someone who preferred to see herself in relation to others, Grace Lee Boggs embodied the gift of her name. She demonstrated grace.

* * *

A few years ago, a student in my African American literature class mentioned that the books I taught painted a picture of Black life so unrelentingly bleak and warped by racism and injustice that a reader might assume all Black life could be reduced to suffering. I was embarrassed that I hadn't seen this, that in trying to teach about Black humanity, I had done the opposite and shown only one limited side of Black life. I had overlooked the everyday moments of joy and agency. As bell hooks writes, "Marginality [is] much more than a site of deprivation. It is also the site of radical possibility, a space of resistance." A site of survivance.

I've written a lot about how my mom was a rage monster and my dad was a starving refugee, and how their lives were One Big Struggle. I realize this can feed into sad immigrant tropes and turn their stories into one-dimensional tragedies. My parents' lives are not tragic. My life is not tragic. We are not uniquely cursed or uniquely blessed. We are exceedingly average, with lives that are full of joy as well as pain.

The stories I've told in this book are ones that I'm sure lots of other Asian Americans, immigrant Americans, women of color, and survivors of war and trauma have experienced.

As Zora Neale Hurston wrote almost a century ago, "I am not tragically colored. No, I do not weep at the world—I am too busy sharpening my oyster knife." Hurston's books are full of unapologetic pleasure. She is not interested in the white world's pity, nor is she interested in packaging Black suffering for a white audience. She is busy living. Sharing her joy with others is a way of connecting beyond trauma, of creating what Audre Lorde calls a "bridge" between the sharers. Her world is abundant and luxuriant and rich, and she possesses the tools to open it up, to harvest its riches— and to defend herself.

I have an oyster knife, too. It's called a pen. And it's very, very sharp.

When I sold this book, I didn't tell my parents right away. I told my friends before I told my parents. I told my sister. I told my husband's parents. I told Twitter. But I didn't tell my own parents. They have never been the people I run to for affirmation or support. They're happy when I do well, and I believe they are proud of me (in their own way). But running to them with good news is usually greeted with confusion or, at the most, mild surprise.

A few days after I signed my book contract, my father sent my sister and me an email:

> Hi Julia & Sharon,
>   We got extra persimmons to share with you. Will you pick them up from my home any time?
>   Dad

I wrote back:

OK Dad!!! I can pick them up tomorrow. I love persimmons.

Also, I just sold a book :) I've attached the announcement.

xoxoxo

My dad didn't respond. I didn't necessarily expect him
to. But a few hours later, he called me.

"I got your email," he said. "You said you sold a book?"

"Yes!" I said. "It's a big deal! It's really hard to sell a book."
(I was shouting, partly to convey my excitement, but partly
because my dad is deaf and never wears his hearing aids.)

"You wrote it already?"

"No, I sold the proposal! I still have to write the book.
That's how it works."

"But you sold a book? One book?"

"Yeah—I didn't get a two-book deal, but that's OK.
Just getting a contract for one book is huge. Dad, it's a big
deal—trust me. It's incredibly hard to get published."

"Oh. OK. Congratulations! So you sold one book." My
father paused. "How much money did you get?" he asked.
"Twenty dollars? Isn't that how much one book usually costs?"

"Put the knife away," the poet Li-Young Lee writes in his
poem "Persimmons." "Lay down newspaper. Peel the skin
tenderly, not to tear the meat."

I'm laying down my knife. I'm offering you the meat of the
oyster. The heart of the persimmon.

* * *

One of my favorite poems to teach is Walt Whitman's "A Noiseless Patient Spider." It's a short poem, just two stanzas, and I find it unusual for Whitman, a larger-than-life figure best known for his exuberant epic poem *Song of Myself* and his glorification of the "I" ("I celebrate myself, and sing myself, and what I assume you shall assume"). Some students love Whitman's showy individuality, others find it grating and solipsistic. I fall somewhere in the middle. Let's just say that Whitman is very white, very male, and very *American*. (His name is Whitman, after all.)

"A Noiseless Patient Spider" is a quieter poem, small and contained where *Song of Myself* is sprawling and loud. It's a different Whitman who appears in this poem, one whom I admit to liking better.

> A noiseless patient spider,
> I mark'd where on a little promontory it stood isolated,
> Mark'd how to explore the vacant vast surrounding,
> It launch'd forth filament, filament, filament, out of itself,
> Ever unreeling them, ever tirelessly speeding them.
>
> And you O my soul where you stand,
> Surrounded, detached, in measureless oceans of space,
> Ceaselessly musing, venturing, throwing, seeking the
>   spheres to connect them,
> Till the bridge you will need be form'd, till the ductile
>   anchor hold,
> Till the gossamer thread you fling catch somewhere, O my
>   soul.

The spider is so, so small. The universe is so, so big. The spider works silently and alone. No one notices its work—no one, that is, except the poet.

Then Whitman pivots, addressing his own soul with such tenderness it makes me cry. Like the spider, Whitman is one tiny soul in the vast universe. He, too, casts out thread after thread, seeking connection in the abyss. How gorgeous a metaphor for the work of the writer or artist—working in anonymity, hoping a filament of their work will catch with a fellow soul in these "measureless oceans of space." The connection is fragile; not all the threads will catch. But the ones that do will form a "ductile anchor," a steely bridge of spiritual connection.

(My son, who has been reading this over my shoulder, interrupts me. He has just finished *Charlotte's Web* in class, and he informs me that spider's silk is actually *stronger* than steel.)

Reading and writing are acts of grace. They connect humans to humans, the individual to the community, the community to the world. Grace is meant to be shared and reciprocated. It is a gift that is passed along, a sacred connection. James Baldwin cast me a line. And Jamaica Kincaid. And Grace Lee Boggs. My teachers cast me a line. My students, too. Together, they formed a network of kinfolk that kept me from falling into the abyss.

Would Whitman have imagined someone like me as his reader? Would he have imagined someone like me catching the thread of his poem? Would he have imagined me as kin? I suspect not, but perhaps this is an opportunity for me to extend him some grace. Sometimes threads catch in unexpected places, O my soul.

I think about Whitman's poem "I Hear America Singing," written on the eve of the Civil War, as the nation was being torn apart over slavery. Whitman depicts the nation as a chorus of white working-class mechanics, farmers, seamstresses, and washerwomen united in song. It's a rousing poem, but it conspicuously elides a whole bunch of other "working" Americans—the Indigenous peoples who first cared for the land, the enslaved peoples who worked on its plantations, the Chinese laborers who built its railroads. Do they not also sing America?

Sixty years later, Langston Hughes caught the thread of Whitman's poem and crafted his own response. The nation was at another moment of racial crisis, facing the rise of Jim Crow, a resurgent Ku Klux Klan, a wave of race riots and lynchings. I am certain Whitman never imagined someone like Hughes—born in Missouri, the descendent of enslaved Africans—reading his poem, much less writing his own. Yet Hughes announces himself as "the darker brother," invisible and ignored by white America, missing from Whitman's poetic vision yet nonetheless *kin*. Relegated to the kitchen, he grows stronger and louder, swells with beauty and abundance and joy, and writes himself into the poem of America:

> They'll see how beautiful I am
> And be ashamed—
>
> I, too, sing America.

A hundred years later, I teach both Whitman and Hughes in my classes. Did they imagine someone like me forming a spiritual or literary or human connection to them?

Did they imagine me as kin? I am forty-six, a woman of Korean descent, born on sacred Gabrielino-Tongva land. The nation is at another moment of racial reckoning. I want to add my voice to the chorus, write myself into this tattered musical brocade, cast my own thread out into the vacant vast surrounding. This book is that attempt.

I hope my fellow souls—my fellow Asian Americans and children of immigrants, Indigenous comrades, colleagues of color, white accomplices, and anyone else who has felt invisible and alone—will catch the thread.

I hope those who I have overlooked or ignored will forgive me and show me grace.

I hope you, my reader, will cast your own threads, tell your own stories, and connect with other souls. Let's build a big, beautiful web of connection and strength.

We, too, are America.

ACKNOWLEDGMENTS

I want to thank my mother, Sonia Meng Soon Kim, and my father, David Eun Sung Lee. Thank you for immigrating, for sacrificing, for buying me persimmons. I also want to thank my sister, Sharon. I would not have survived childhood without you.

I honor the memory of Soon Chung Park, Hyun Jung Park, Suncha Kim, Yong Yue, Xiaojie Tan, Daoyou Feng, and all victims of anti-Asian brutality and violence.

I honor the memory of Latasha Harlins, Rodney King, George Floyd, Breonna Taylor, Tamir Rice, Michael Brown, Trayvon Martin, and all victims of anti-Black brutality and violence.

I acknowledge the Gabrielino-Tongva people on whose unceded land my parents settled and I now live. I honor the ancestors, elders, and kinfolk past, present, and emerging.

The one good thing about holding grudges is that I also always remember acts of kindness. Thank you to my teachers and mentors, who cast me a line when I felt most alone, especially Jamaica Kincaid, Skip Gates, Elaine Scarry, Lisa Sternlieb, Sister Mary Enda, Nancy McCarthy, Ric Kajikawa, Anne-Marie Jenks, Deborah Nord, Maria DiBattista, Gwee-Sook Kim, and Janet Tunick.

Thank you to the Sonneborns, the Malkiels, and the Bachs for welcoming me into their families.

I would not have survived high school without Sharon Gi, Riva Kim, Lizzy Castruccio, Grace Choi, Chris Lau Corey, Lydia Cho, and Tarry Baker Payton. I would not have survived college without Sandhya Gupta, Miki Terasawa, Jennifer Heckart, Mony Singh, Maria Wich-Vila, Kitlyn Seto, Terri Sesay, Bob Chen, and Evonne Johnson. I would not have survived grad school and beyond without Manoucheka Celeste, Laura Murphy, Ashley Howard, Kate Bonnici, and David Roh.

To my colleagues, especially Jae Williams, Mairead Sullivan, Jenny Ferguson, Linh Hua, and all the members of the LMU Teaching Toward Justice group—you are my beloved community. To Melanie Hubbard, Alex Neel, Robin Miskolcze, Tara Pixley, Kate Pickert, Evelyn McDonnell, Juan Mah y Busch, Stuart Ching, Rubén Martinez, KJ Peters, Barbara Rico, John Reilly, Nadia Kim, Ed Park, Curtiss Takada Rooks, Denise Tillery, Miriam Melton-Villanueva, Anne Stevens, Emily Setina, Vince Perez, Suzy Newbury, Melody Mansfield, and Rhonda Rockwell: I am honored to work with you. Jane Hafen, thank you for being my teacher, colleague, and friend.

To my students, past and present, for helping me see things anew—especially Taylore Fox, Tyler Dunson, Sin À Tes Souhaits, Hayley Dennings, Ashley Munoz, Yoán Moreno, Mauricio Hernandez, Angelo Antonio, Rae Lontok, Alana

Fa'agai, Rosie Vargas, Camille Morris, Elsha Harris-Yolanda, Camila Hernandez-Quintero, and so many more. I especially want to thank my Spring 2022 Asian American literature class at LMU, who helped me think through many of the ideas in this book.

Thank you to Ruby Rose Lee, for being the editor I had always dreamed of but was told might not exist. Anita Sheih—thank you for shepherding this book through its final stages and for your sense of humor in responding to my random emails. To Lynn Wu, thank you for reading with an open heart and connecting with the manuscript. Many thanks to my agent, Liza Dawson, and to my former agent, Jennifer Johnson-Blalock. In many ways, I have been trying to write this book since I was thirteen years old. Thank you for believing that I have something to say.

My children, Lucy and Bobby, have inherited the righteous rage of their ancestors. I hope this book helps you understand where this gift comes from. My dogs, Moose and Lucky, and my cats, Ollie, Warren, and Pineapple, daily prove that animals are better than people. Thanks for keeping me company as I wrote on the couch. Finally, to my husband, Brad—thank you for your love and grace. You are definitely my mother's favorite child.

ABOUT THE AUTHOR

Julia Lee is a Korean American writer, scholar, and teacher. She is the author of *"Our Gang": A Racial History of "The Little Rascals"* and *The American Slave Narrative and the Victorian Novel*, as well as the novel *By the Book*. She is an associate professor of English at Loyola Marymount University, where she teaches African American and Caribbean literature. She lives with her family in Los Angeles.